# shepherds of Christ
## N E W S L E T T E R S

*Selected Writings*
*On Spirituality*
*— For All People —*
*As Published in*
*"Shepherds of Christ"*
*Newsletter for Priests*

Rev. Edward J. Carter, S.J., Editor

Shepherds of Christ Publications
Morrow, Ohio

In conformity with the decrees of Pope Urban VIII, the Publisher recognizes and accepts that the final authority regarding the messages of private revelation rests with the Holy See of Rome, to whose judgment we willingly submit.

—*The Publisher*

Imprimi Potest: Bradley M. Schaeffer, S.J.

Nihil Obstat:    Rev. Robert J. Buschmiller

Imprimatur:     Carl K. Moeddel
                Auxiliary Bishop
                Archdiocese of Cincinnati

This book is published by Shepherds of Christ Publications, a subsidiary of Shepherds of Christ Ministries, a tax exempt religious public charitable association organized to foster devotion to the Two Hearts, the Sacred Heart of Jesus and the Immaculate Heart of Mary.

For additional copies, write to:
  Shepherds of Christ Publications
  P.O. Box 193
  Morrow, Ohio 45152-0193

### Acknowledgements
The editor acknowledges the use of certain book excerpts as follows:
From *The Jerusalem Bible* by Alexander Jones, ed., © 1966 by Darton, Longman & Todd, Ltd. and Doubleday, a division of Bantam Doubleday Dell Publishing Group, Inc. Used by permission of Doubleday, a division of Doubleday, a division of Bantam Doubleday Dell Publishing Group, Inc.
From the English translation of *The Liturgy of the Hours* © 1974, International Committee on English in the Liturgy, Inc. All rights reserved.
From *The Documents of Vatican II,* reprinted with permission of America Press, Inc., 106 West 56th Street, New York, New York 10019, © 1966. All rights reserved.
From *Called to Serve, Called to Lead* by Archbishop Joseph Bernardin, © 1981 by St. Anthony Messenger Press, 1615 Republic Street, Cincinnati, OH 45210. Reprinted with permission.

First Printing: April, 1997

# Contents

# Introduction

The pages which follow are those which made up the first twelve issues of the spirituality newsletter for priests entitled *Shepherds of Christ.* We think it valuable that priests are able to have all these newsletters available in one, compact volume. As we state in the *Editor's Corner* column of the first issue:

> *The purpose of this spirituality newsletter for priests is to offer yet another aid to priests in the development of their spiritual lives. We live in very critical times for both the Church and the world. We priests, by our very vocation, are in a most advantageous position to make an extremely significant contribution to the betterment of both Church and world. And the more we ourselves grow spiritually according to the Gospel message, the more we are able to help the Church and the world progress according to God's will.*

The subtitle of this book is *Selected Writings on Spirituality—for All People—as Published in Shepherds of Christ Newsletter for Priests.* Consequently, we offer the following pages to all. Although some entries are aimed specifically at priests, the overwhelming percentage of the material can hopefully be used by all those interested in growth in the spiritual life.

Before readers progress to the pages of the various issues of the newsletters, we think it valuable to offer a brief overview of one's spiritual journey in Christ.

## An Overview of the Spiritual Life

The Christian life is rooted in the great event of the Incarnation. We must consequently always focus our gaze upon Christ, realizing that everything the Father wishes to tell us has been summed up in the life, death, and resurrection of Jesus. It only remains for us, then, to strive to understand with greater insight the inexhaustible truth of the Word Incarnate (Heb 1:1-2).

What was the condition of the human race at the time of Christ's coming? In some ways, people were much the same as we are today. There were those just being born into this world of human drama. There were those who, in death, were leaving it, some of whom had grasped but little of life's meaning. There were those who were healthy and vigorous. There were those who were sick and lame. Some especially felt the burdens, the grief, the suffering of the human condition. Others were ebullient and desired all the pleasures life could provide. There was some good being accomplished. Immorality, however, was rampant. What St. Paul tells us concerning the time that immediately followed Christ's existence certainly could also be applied to the time of His entrance into the world. It is, in short, an ugly picture that St. Paul depicts for us (Rom 1:22-32).

Into such a depraved condition Jesus entered, with a full and generous Heart, to lead the human race from the depths of sinfulness to the vibrant richness of a new life in Himself. Through His enfleshment, this Christ became the focal point of all history. The authentic hopes and dreams of the human family, now so overshadowed by the ugliness of sin, came converging upon this Christ. He would gather them up in Himself, give them a new luster and brilliance and dynamism, and would lead the human family back to the Father in the Holy Spirit.

Christ was radically to release us from the dominion of sin and elevate us to a new level of existence. This life Christ has given us is not a type of superstructure which is erected atop human existence. Although nature and grace are distinct, they do not lie side by side as separate entities. Rather, grace permeates nature. The Christian is one graced person. The Christian is one who has been raised up, caught up, into a deeper form of life in Christ Jesus. Nothing that is authentically human in the life of the Christian has been excluded from this new existence. Whatever is really human in the life of the Christian is meant to be an expression of the Christ-life. The simple but deep joys of family life, the wonderment at nature's beauty, the warm embrace of a mother for her child, the agony of crucial decision making, the success or frustration that is experienced in one's work, the joy of being well received by others, and the heartache of being misunderstood—all these experiences are intended to be caught up in Christ and made more deeply human because of Him.

Jesus has come, then, not to destroy anything that is authentically human, but to perfect it by leading it to a graced fulfillment. The more God-like we become through Christ, the more human we become.

We, through our incorporation into Christ which occurs at Baptism, are meant to relive the life, death, and resurrection of Jesus. In doing so, we are not only accomplishing our own salvation, but we are assisting in the salvation of others also. The Incarnation continues all the time. Christ, or course, is the one Who fundamentally continues the Incarnation. But He enlists our help. The world no longer sees Jesus, no longer is able to reach out and touch Him. We are the ones who now, in some way, make Christ visible and tangible. In union with the invisible, glorified Christ, and depending on Him as our source of life, we continue the Incarnation in its visible and temporal dimensions. This is our great privilege. This is our great responsibility.

The Christian is initiated into the mystery of Christ, into his or her role in prolonging the Incarnation, through Baptism (Rom 6:3-4).

It is not sufficient, however, that we be incorporated into Christ through Baptism. All forms of life require nourishment. So, too, our life in Christ must be continually nourished. How can we continually keep in contact with

Christ? There are various ways. We contact Christ in a most special way through the liturgy, above all in the Eucharistic liturgy. Through our most special and most personal meeting with Jesus in the Mass, we are more deeply incorporated into Christ. Also, we should remember that all the sacraments make up part of the Church's liturgy.

The reading of Scripture provides another special opportunity for meeting Jesus. This is true for both Old and New Testaments. The Old Testament prefigures the New Testament and leads to it. It is obvious, however, that we meet Christ especially in the pages of the New Testament. How true it is to say that not to be familiar with Scripture is not to know Jesus properly. We should resolve to read from Scripture daily.

We also meet Jesus in our interaction with others. Everyone we meet, everyone we serve, is in the image of Jesus. We have to take the means to grow in this awareness. If I truly believe that everyone has been redeemed by the blood of Jesus, how should I treat everyone?

These, then, are some of the ways we keep in contact with Jesus. Common to the various ways of meeting Jesus is a certain degree of prayerful reflection. Our contact with Jesus in the liturgy, in Scripture, and in our interaction with others, and so forth, will not be all that it should be unless we are persons of prayer. The light and strength of prayer enables us to keep in contact with Jesus as we should.

We live out our Christ-life in an atmosphere of love. Indeed, the life Jesus has given us is centered in love. It has its origins in the mysterious love of God (Jn 3:16).

Our new life in Jesus has arisen out of God's fathomless love. Christ, in His descent into human flesh, has established a milieu of love. The life He came to give can flourish only in the framework of love. Indeed, we can summarize the meaning of the Christian life by stating that it is our loving response to God's love. The pierced Heart of Jesus, this Heart which shed its last drop of blood in the greatest love for each one of us, is the symbol of God's tremendous love for us. Christ's Heart also calls us to respond by giving ourselves in love to God and neighbor. Yes, Jesus invites us to respond to God's love by giving ourselves in love to Him in an ever closer union. The more closely we are united to Him, the greater is our capacity to love God and neighbor. The more closely we are united with Jesus, the more closely He unites us to the Father in the Holy Spirit, with Mary our Mother at our side.

May the ideas contained in this brief overview of the spiritual life be deepened and expanded through the reading of the following pages.

> Fr. Edward J. Carter, S.J.
> Professor of Theology, Xavier University,
> and Spiritual Director of Shepherds of Christ Ministries

A Publication of
Shepherds of Christ
Ministries

# shepherds of Christ

## A SPIRITUALITY NEWSLETTER FOR PRIESTS

**JULY/AUGUST 1994**

# Chief Shepherd of the Flock

I am the Good Shepherd: the Good Shepherd is one who lays down His life for His sheep. The hired man, since he is not the shepherd and the sheep do not belong to him, abandons the sheep and runs away as soon as he sees a wolf coming, and then the wolf attacks and scatters the sheep. This is because he is only a hired man and has no concern for the sheep. I am the Good Shepherd. I know My own and My own know Me, just as the Father knows Me and I know the Father. And I lay down My life for My sheep. (Jn 10: 11-15[1]).

He hung upon a cross on a hill called Calvary. Death was near. How much Jesus had already suffered! He had been brutally scourged. Much of His sacred body was a bloody, open wound. He had been derisively crowned with thorns. In a terribly weakened condition, He carried the heavy cross to the hill of Golgotha. There He was stripped of His garments and mercilessly nailed to the cross. After all this brutal and agonizing suffering, Jesus finally died.

Truly, the Good Shepherd had laid down His life for His sheep. That magnificent Heart, overflowing with love for His Father and all of us, had beat Its last:

"It was Preparation Day, and to prevent the bodies remaining on the cross during the sabbath—since that sabbath was a day of special solemnity—the Jews asked Pilate to have the legs broken and the bodies taken away. Consequently the soldiers came and broke the legs of the first man who had been crucified with him and then of the other. When they came to Jesus, they found He was already dead, and so instead of breaking His legs one of the soldiers pierced His side with a lance. And immediately there came out blood and water." (Jn 19: 31-34).

Indeed, from the pierced Heart of Christ the Church with her sacraments was born. Two of these sacraments, the Eucharist and Baptism, are symbolized by the blood and water flowing from Christ's side. The sacrament of Orders was, of course, also born from the pierced Heart of Christ. We who

See *Chief Shepherd*, page 2, bottom

1

# Editor's Corner
by Edward Carter S.J.

My dear fellow priests,

We wish to say a very warm and cordial hello to all our fellow priests! This is our first issue of *Shepherds of Christ,* and it is, indeed, a real pleasure to come into your company through the printed word.

The purpose of this spirituality newsletter for priests is to offer yet another aid to priests in the development of their spiritual lives. We live in very critical times for both the Church and the world. We priests, by our very vocation, are in a most advantageous position to make an extremely significant contribution to the betterment of both Church and world. And the more we ourselves grow spiritually according to the Gospel message, the more we are able to help the Church and the world progress according to God's will.

The newsletter will be sent to you six times yearly, free of charge. However, we certainly very much appreciate your donations to help cover the cost of printing and mailing.

Finally, we invite you to send us your comments and observations. *Shepherds of Christ* is your newsletter, and we want it to be a newsletter which speaks as effectively as possible to you concerning growth in the priestly way of spiritual life.

---

*Chief Shepherd* continued from page 1

are priests can never adequately thank Jesus for allowing us to receive this great and most special sacrament. The best way we can try to thank Him, though, is to utilize our priesthood to the fullest. We priests have the great privilege and the great responsibility of being special companions of the Chief Shepherd of the flock, Jesus Himself.

Jesus laid down His life for His sheep. Being shepherds of the Chief Shepherd we, too, are called to lay down our lives for the flock. Relatively few priests in the course of the Church's history have been called to lay down their lives in physical martyrdom. All, though, have been and are called to lay down their lives for the flock by giving themselves in loving service according to the Father's will.

We are effective shepherds to the extent we are united with Christ. Let's resolve each day of our priestly existence to utilize all the means available to deepen our union with Jesus, Chief Shepherd of the flock.

# Notes from a Karl Rahner Retreat

The following is an excerpt from notes taken during a retreat given by Father Karl Rahner, one of the most eminent theologians of our time. The retreat was given to a group of candidates for the priesthood. The notes were edited and put into book form.

"Really only a *holy* priest is neither a mere religious functionary nor an overly zealous religious fanatic. He is not bitter in spite of the true bitterness of human existence. He does not try to escape into neurotic extravagances. He is able to persevere patiently with God and to accept from Him his vocation to follow Christ as a priest without demanding the same thing from everyone else. The holy priest knows how to give things up, pure and simple, without tarnishing his relationship to the world. He can give up everything because he truly loves God and finds everything again in Him. We are on the way toward this type of priestly existence—with God' grace—and our concrete life is a mixture of its basic elements. And we should have confidence that the God who couples His incalculable call to the priesthood onto the common religious tendency will also bring to completion in us the good work that He began."[2]

In the above passage, Rahner reminds us of the necessity of holiness for the priest. Some misconstrue what holiness is. Holiness is simply leading the God-life of grace—received at Baptism—as best as one can with the help of God's ongoing gift of graces. And since this life of grace, which is a participation in Trinitarian life, is given to us through the mediation of Christ, this grace-life has a Christlike structure. In other words, the call to holiness is the call to put on Christ, to follow Christ as closely as possible. Each day let us strive to know Christ more intimately, to love Him more ardently, and to follow Him more closely. If we live in this manner, we are growing in the life of holiness.

# The Theology of Consecration

A. Boussard gives an extremely fine and concise sketch of the theology of consecration:

"By the Incarnation, in and of itself, the Humanity of Jesus is consecrated, so that in becoming Man, Jesus is ipso facto constituted Savior, Prophet, King, Priest, and Victim of the One Sacrifice that was to save the world. He is the 'Anointed', par excellence, the 'Christ' totally belonging to God, His Humanity being that of the Word and indwelled by the Holy Spirit. When, by a free act of His human will, He accepts what He is, doing what He was sent to do, He can say that He consecrates 'Himself'. In Christ, therefore, what might be called His 'subjective' consecration is a perfect response to the 'objective' consecration produced in His Humanity through the Incarnation.

"And what Christ does brings with it is a 'consecration' for His disciples, a very special belonging to God, since He imparts to them His own life precisely by making them participate in His own consecration.

"Through Baptism Christians also are consecrated and 'anointed' by the power of the Spirit. They share, in their measure, in the essential consecration of Christ, in His character of King, Priest, and Prophet (cf. 1 Peter 2:9; 7 Peter 1:3-4; Rev. 5:9, etc.). With Christ and through Christ, they are 'ordered' to the glory of God and the salvation of the world. They do not belong to themselves. They belong to Christ the Lord, who imparts His own life to them...

"The vocation of those who have been baptized is to 'live' this consecration by a voluntary adherence—and one that is as perfect as possible—to what it has made of them. Living as 'children of God', they fulfill subjectively their objective consecration; like Jesus, they consecrate themselves. This is the deeper meaning of vows and baptismal promises, together with the actual way of life corresponding to them. The baptismal consecration is the fundamental one, constitutive of the Christian. All consecrations which come after it presuppose and are rooted in it..."[3]

# Act of Priestly Consecration

Lord Jesus, Chief Shepherd of the flock, I consecrate my priestly life to Your most Sacred Heart. From Your pierced Heart the Church was born, the Church You have called me, as a priest, to serve in a most special way. You reveal Your Heart as symbol of Your love in all its aspects including Your most special love for me, whom You have chosen as Your priest-companion. Help me always to love You in return. Help me to give myself entirely to You. Help me always to pour out my life in love of God and neighbor. Heart of Jesus, I place my trust in You!

Dear Blessed Virgin Mary, I consecrate myself to your maternal and Immaculate Heart, this Heart which is symbol of your life of love. You are the Mother of my Savior. You are also my Mother. You love me with a most special love as this unique priest-son. In a return of love, I give myself entirely to your motherly love and protection. You followed Jesus perfectly. You are His first and perfect disciple. Teach me to imitate you in the putting on of Christ. Be my motherly intercessor that, through your Immaculate Heart, I may be guided to an ever closer union with the pierced Heart of Jesus, Chief Shepherd of the flock.

# The New Catechism and Thoughts on the Priesthood

Here are some inspiring words on the priesthood from the new Catholic Catechism:

"Before the grandeur of the priestly grace and office, the holy doctors felt an urgent call to conversion in order to conform their whole lives to him whose sacrament had made them ministers. Thus St. Gregory of Nazianzus, as a very young priest, exclaimed:

"'We must begin by purifying ourselves before purifying others; we must be instructed to be able to instruct, become light to illuminate, draw close to God to bring him close to others, be sanctified to sanctify, lead by the hand and counsel prudently. I know whose ministers we are, where we find ourselves and to where we strive. I know God's greatness and man's weakness, but also his potential. (Who then is the priest? He is) the defender of truth, who stands with angels, gives glory with archangels, causes sacrifices to rise to the altar on high, shares Christ's priesthood, refashions creation, restores it in God's image, recreates it for the world on high and, even greater, is divinized and divinizes.'"[4]

# Vatican II on the Priesthood

Vatican II reminds us of the purpose of our being priests, of being shepherds of Christ, Who is Chief Shepherd of the flock:

"The purpose, therefore, which priests pursue by their ministry and life is the glory of God the Father as it is to be achieved in Christ. That glory consists in this: that men knowingly, freely, and gratefully accept what God has achieved perfectly through Christ, and manifest it in their whole lives. Hence, whether engaged in prayer and adoration, preaching the Word, offering the Eucharistic sacrifice, ministering the other sacraments, or performing any of the other works of the ministry for men, priests are contributing to the extension of God's glory as well as to the development of divine life in men."[5]

# Messages from Jesus and Mary

(We recognize and accept that the final authority regarding these messages rests with the Holy See of Rome, to whose judgment we willingly submit. The decree of the Congregation for the Propagation of the Faith, A.A.S.

---

6       SHEPHERDS OF CHRIST NEWSLETTERS

58, 1186, approved by Pope Paul VI on October 14, 1966, states that the Imprimatur is no longer required on publications that deal with new revelations, apparitions, prophesies or miracles. It is presumed such publications contain nothing contrary to faith and morals.—*The Editor.*)

## Message of Our Lady of Medjugorje

"Dear children, today I am calling you to complete surrender to God. Everything you do and everything you possess give over to God so that He can take control in your life as King of all that you possess. That way, through me, God can lead you into the depths of the spiritual life..."[6]

## Message of Jesus

"I love My priests with an overwhelming, burning love! I have given them the great privilege and great responsibility of acting in My name in a most special way. In My great love for My priests, I call them to the highest holiness.

"Let them not be afraid of the call to holiness. I give them abundant graces to grow in holiness. They must resolve to respond to these graces. They must resolve to use the means to grow in holiness. The Mass must be the center of their lives. They must pray much, including the daily recitation of the Liturgy of the Hours. At least some of their prayer should be made before the Tabernacle, where I grant special graces. Nor should they neglect the other ordinary means for the pursuit of holiness.

"I love each of My priests with a most special love! Each day I call them by name. Each day, I call them to come, in union with Mary, to My Heart. I ask them to dwell within My Heart. Here I will give them a sense of My great love for them. Here I will enlighten and strengthen them regarding their priestly ministry. Here I will give them special peace and joy. I am Lord and Master! I urgently request that My priests answer My call. In My great and special love for them, I give them this message!"[7]

## Message of Jesus

"Trust in Me, My child...Open yourself up to Me and trust. Why do you not see that Satan wants to stop you and that he does not want the world to get these messages. Such messages of love and comfort! If he can work on you, you will stop. Don't be fooled by him. He is the great deceiver. He plans to trip you up...You, My child, are strong in Me. I need you to do My work. Laboring in your head, looking for proof, not totally trusting in Me—those come from him. Step on his head. Open your heart to Me and My love—no room for a drop of doubt. I am truly here talking to you, little one. Think about My passion and death. I loved you. I love you this much still today. My heart is so on fire for love of you. You can't even begin to know how much love I have for you. Just be open to all I send you and cast your doubts away. It is your act of trusting that helps you develop trust in Me. Step-by-step you ascend the stairs and you get closer each time to trusting more in Me. It is your taking each little step that counts. Ascend My steps each day, every day. A million times a day you can trust or worry. You choose, 'Do I trust or not trust?' How could you not trust after all I did to prove My love for you? Focus on My passion, on My wounds, on My love, on Me..."[8]

## NOTES

1. Scriptural quotations are taken from *The Jerusalem Bible*, Doubleday & Co.
2. Karl Rahner, S.J., *Spiritual Exercises*, Herder & Herder, pg. 155.
3. A. Boussard in *Dictionary of Mary*, Catholic Book Publishing Co., pp. 54-55.
4. *The Catechism of the Catholic Church*, pg. 397.
5. *The Documents of Vatican II*, Decree on the Ministry and Life of Priests, No. 2, America Press edition.
6. Message of Our Lady of Medjugorje, July 25, 1988, as contained in Daniel Golob's *Live the Messages*, The Riehle Foundation.
7. Message of Jesus to a chosen one.
8. *God's Blue Book*, messages received by Rita Ring, Our Lady of Light Publications, pg. 52.

A Publication of
Shepherds of Christ
Ministries

# shepherds of Christ

## A SPIRITUALITY NEWSLETTER FOR PRIESTS

SEPTEMBER/OCTOBER 1994

# Chief Shepherd of the Flock

I am the Good Shepherd: the Good Shepherd is one who lays down His life for His sheep. The hired man, since he is not the shepherd and the sheep do not belong to him, abandons the sheep and runs away as soon as he sees a wolf coming, and then the wolf attacks and scatters the sheep. This is because he is only a hired man and has no concern for the sheep. I am the Good Shepherd. I know My own and My own know Me, just as the Father knows Me and I know the Father. And I lay down My life for My sheep. (Jn 10: 11-15[1]).

A faithful shepherd takes care of his sheep in all their needs. This includes providing them with the proper food. Jesus, the perfect Shepherd, abundantly provides for the nourishment of His flock. In the Eucharist He gives Himself in His body, blood, soul, and divinity for our spiritual growth. He also feeds us through His word, through His teaching. The gospel of John, in chapter 6: 35-59, combines both of these ways—Christ nourishing us through His teaching and through the Eucharist. This particular section of John's gospel gives us Jesus' great discourse on the Bread of Life. The first part, verses 35-50, speaks of the teaching of Jesus as nourishment, as the bread of life. This first part contains, therefore, the so-called sapiential theme. The second part, verses 51-59, speaks of the Eucharist as our heavenly nourishment. This part, therefore, contains the sacramental theme.

Both aspects of the Bread of Life theme reveal God's tremendous love for us. The Eucharist is the sacrament of Jesus' great love for us, and His teaching is summed up in terms of love—God's overwhelming love for us and our duty to love God and neighbor in return. Each day we should pray for an increased realization of how much God, in Christ Jesus, loves each of us with a most special, unique love. Growing in this awareness and living according to this awareness are the keys to growth in the spiritual life. The more we are convinced of how much Christ loves us as unique individuals, the more able are we to enter into a deep love relationship with Jesus. And if we have the proper love relationship with Jesus, everything else falls into

See *Chief Shepherd,* page 10, bottom

## Editor's Corner

by Edward Carter S.J.

Hello again! We hope the vast majority of you received the first issue of Shepherds of Christ. For whatever reasons, some apparently did not receive their copies. For those who did not, we briefly restate a few remarks concerning this spiritual newsletter for priests. We offer it as yet another aid to priests in the development of their spiritual lives. The newsletter will be sent to you six times yearly, free of charge. However, we certainly very much appreciate your donations to help cover the cost of printing and mailing. We also invite your comments and observations.

Yes, we offer this newsletter as yet another aid to help us live our priesthood as true shepherds of Christ. And in these complex times we need all the help we can get!

There are many conditions in today's Church and world which can lead a priest into a state of ongoing discouragement if he does not mount a counteroffensive. And his plan of action must be rooted in his personal relationship with Jesus, this Jesus Who loves each of us with an unfathomable love. Let us always remember the words of St. Paul: "Nothing therefore can come between us and the love of Christ, even if we are troubled or worried, or being persecuted, or lacking food or clothes, or being threatened or even attacked...

"For I am certain of this: neither death nor life, no angel, no prince, nothing that exists, nothing still to come, not any power, or height or depth, nor any created thing, can ever come between us and the love of God made visible in Christ Jesus our Lord." (Rom. 8: 35-39).

---

*Chief Shepherd* continued from page 9

place. Yes, as our union with Jesus grows, He leads us, amid all the pain and all the joy, to a closer union with the Father in the Holy Spirit with Mary, our Mother, at our side.

# Cardinal Bernardin On Priests as Shepherds

"One of the most beautiful images of Christ is that of shepherd. In chapter 10 of John's gospel Jesus calls Himself the good shepherd and explains what this means. The good shepherd, He says, finds pasture for his sheep; he brings back to the fold those who have strayed; if necessary, he lays down his life for them…

"The image of shepherd supports and enriches the concept of priest as servant. The Bishop's Committee on Priestly Life and Ministry strongly emphasized this concept in *As One Who Serves*. The priest, the committee stated, 'is to be a servant of the People of God, holding them accountable for what they have been and can be. He serves them by calling forth leadership and coordinating ministries. His is a service which calls the people to remember and to celebrate the presence and power of the Risen Lord. In the fullest sense, he is a servant of the human family.'

"Our hearts must be moved with pity when we see people who are suffering, whose lives are empty, who are searching vainly for meaning. Through our ministry and our presence, we must do all we can to bring them the riches of the gospel, so that they will come to know the Lord and experience His love and peace in their lives. This is the shepherd's work. This is *our* work as priests who follow in the footsteps of the Good Shepherd and carry on His mission.

"A priest, because of the Person he represents and the message he brings, is one whose ministry is expected to bring people joy, consolation, and hope. Admittedly, a priest cannot remove all the pain and frustration which are part of the human condition. But this ministry can help people cope better with trials and sufferings by seeing them in the light of the Transcendent. While we are obliged to do all we can to promote a better life in this world by building a society rooted in justice and love, in the final analysis our earthly accomplishments and their immediate joys and sorrows are transitory. The ultimate fulfillment of all we attempt, the lasting remedy for all we suffer, lies in life eternal.

"My personal experience convinces me that what people actually want and need is usually much less complex and spectacular than we sometimes imagine. People are not looking for religious leaders who can solve all their problems or answer all their questions. Often they know the answers already; or they know their problem has no immediate solution. More than anything else, people look to us who minister to them for our presence as loving, caring, and forgiving people. They want our help in their efforts to handle pain and frustration. They look to us for understanding; they seek a sensitive and consoling response to their hurt feelings; they need the spiritual comfort we can bring through our ministry of word and sacrament. They want someone who will pray with them, whose presence will remind them that, no matter what their difficulties might be, God really loves them and cares for them. They want assurance that God will never abandon them. This is the preferred style of spiritual leadership in our day."[2]

# Henri Nouwen On
# Union With Jesus

Fr. Henri Nouwen has been one of the most influential spiritual writers of our times. His following words emphasize the overwhelming importance of the Christian leader—and as priests we are certainly called to be leaders—to be intimately united with Jesus:

"Christian leaders cannot simply be persons who have well-informed opinions about the burning issues of our times. Their leadership must be rooted in the permanent, intimate relationship with the incarnate Word, Jesus, and they need to find there the source for their words, advice, and guidance. Through the discipline of contemplative prayer, Christian leaders have to learn to listen again and again to the voice of love and to find there the wisdom and courage to address whatever issue presents itself to them. Dealing with burning issues without being rooted in a deep personal relationship with God easily leads to divisiveness because, before we know it, our sense of self is caught up in our opinion about a given subject. But when we are securely rooted in personal intimacy with the source of life, it will be possible to remain flexible without being relativistic, convinced without being rigid, willing to confront without being offensive, gentle and forgiving without being soft, and true witnesses without being manipulative."[3]

# St. John Eudes On
# Union With Jesus

The following words of St. John Eudes remind us of the glorious goal the Christian is called to: the most intimate union with Jesus. We, as priests, have the special privilege and responsibility of seeking this union with Christ in the highest degree:

"I ask you to consider that our Lord Jesus Christ is your true head and that you are a member of his body. He belongs to you as the head belongs to the body. All that is his is yours: breath, heart, body, soul and all his faculties. All these you must use as if they belonged to you, so that in serving him you may give him praise, love and glory. You belong to him as a member belongs to the head. This is why he earnestly desires you to serve and glorify the Father by using all your faculties as if they were his.

"He belongs to you, but more than that, he longs to be in you, living and ruling in you, as the head lives and rules in the body. He desires that whatever is in him may live and rule in you: his breath in your breath, his heart in your heart, all the faculties of his soul in the faculties of your soul, so that these words may be fulfilled in you: *Glorify God and bear him in your body, that the life of Jesus may be made manifest in you.*

"You belong to the Son of God, but more than that, you ought to be in him as members are in the head. All that is in you must be incorporated into him. You must receive life from him and be ruled by him. There will be no true life for you except in him, for he is the one source of true life. Apart from him you will find only death and destruction. Let him be the only source of your movements, of the actions and the strength of your life. He must be both the source and the purpose of your life, so that you may fulfill these words: *None of us lives as his own master and none of us dies as his own master. While we live, we are responsible to the Lord, and when we die, we die as his servants. Both in life and in death we are the Lord's. That is why Christ died and came to life again, that he might be Lord of both the dead and the living.*

"Finally, you are one with Jesus as the body is one with the head. You must, then, have one breath with him, one soul, one life, one will, one mind, one heart. And he must be your breath, heart, love, life, your all. These great gifts in the follower of Christ originate from baptism. They are increased and strengthened through confirmation and by making good use of other graces that are given by God. Through the holy eucharist they are brought to perfection."[4]

# Karl Rahner On The Imitation of Christ

The following is an excerpt from notes taken during a retreat given by Fr. Karl Rahner, S.J. The retreat was given to a group of candidates for the priesthood. The notes were edited into book form: "We should not reduce participation in the life of Jesus to some sort of moral relationship. Moral influence coming from Jesus must be made possible by and based on an ontological influence. By reason of the Incarnation of the Word and the whole history of the life and death of Jesus, each of us is already personally involved in the life of Jesus. In fact the whole world including the life of every human being is really affected and determined by His human existence. In a narrower and historically perceptible sense, after being affected by Him we are incorporated by Baptism into that community which is His Body, and by this sacramental-ontological determination of our historical existence, we were drawn even further into His life...

"The imitation of Christ consists in a true entering into *His* life and *in Him* entering into the inner life of the God that has been given to us."[5]

# St. Teresa of Avila
# On Doing God's Will

The close union with Jesus which Henri Nouwen, St. John Eudes, and Karl Rahner talk about centers in our doing Christ's will out of love for Him. Jesus' will for us is, of course, the same as His Father's will for us. St. Teresa of Avila, one of the two women doctors of the Church (the other is St. Catherine of Siena) tells us how the spiritual life is summed up in loving conformity to God's will:

"All that the beginner in prayer has to do—and you must not forget this, for it is very important—is to labor and to be resolute and prepare himself with all possible diligence to bring his will in conformity with the will of God. As I shall say later, you may be quite sure that this comprises the very greatest perfection which can be attained on the spiritual road."[6] Again she states: "…love consists…in the firmness of our determination to try to please God in everything."[7]

# John Powell On Saying
# "Yes" to the Will of God

A very popular spiritual writer of our time, Fr. John Powell, S.J., gives us thoughts concerning saying "yes" to God's will. His words easily follow the above thoughts of St. Teresa:

"There have been quite a few times in my life when I have felt the winds of God's grace in the sails of my small boat. Sometimes these graces have moved me in pleasant and sunlit directions. At other times the requested acts of love were born in darkness of struggle and suffering. There have been springtimes and there have been long, cold winters of struggle for survival. God has come to me at times with the purest kindness, at times with the most affirming encouragement, and at other times with bold and frightening challenges. I think that all of us have to watch and pray, to be ready to say 'yes' when God's language is concrete and his request is specific—'yes' in the sunlit springtimes and 'yes' in the darkness of winter nights."[8]

# St. Louis de Montfort
# On Consecration

A contemporary Marian scholar, Fr. Arthur Collins, offers the following thought concerning St. Louis de Montfort, one of the greatest of Marian apostles: "Perhaps, in the final analysis, the greatest contribution of this Breton saint to the theology of Marian consecration is precisely in his insistence on Mary's mediation as willed by God."[9]

St. Louis de Montfort himself sums up, in a few words, his thoughts on consecration, "The more one is consecrated to Mary, the more one is consecrated to Jesus."[10]

# A Priestly Consecration

The previously quoted words of St. John Eudes remind us of the extremely close union we are called to have with Jesus. As we realize Jesus' tremendous and most special unique love for each of us, we are asked to give ourselves in a return of love to Jesus. We are called to strive to live the union described by St. John Eudes. In other words, we are called to continue to say "yes" to the objective consecration we received in the sacraments of Baptism and Holy Orders. There follows a suggested act of consecration:

Lord Jesus, Chief Shepherd of the flock, I consecrate my priestly life to your most Sacred Heart. From Your pierced Heart the Church was born, the Church You have called me, as a priest, to serve in a most special way. You reveal Your Heart as symbol of Your love in all its aspects, including Your most special love for me, whom You have chosen as Your priest-companion. Help me always to give myself entirely to You. Help me always to pour out my life in love of God and neighbor. Heart of Jesus, I place my trust in You!

Dear Blessed Virgin Mary, I consecrate myself to your maternal and Immaculate Heart, this Heart which is symbol of your life of love. You are the Mother of my Savior. You are also my Mother. You love me with a most special love as this unique priest-son. In a return of love, I give myself entirely to your motherly love and protection. You followed Jesus perfectly. You are his first and perfect disciple. Teach me to imitate you in the putting on of Christ. Be my motherly intercessor that, through your Immaculate Heart, I may be guided to an ever closer union with the pierced Heart of Jesus, Chief Shepherd of the Flock.

# Shepherds of Christ Associates

We have started a spiritual movement which has a connection with this particular newsletter. The movement is called Shepherds of Christ Associates. The associates belong to groups, or chapters. These groups meet on a regular basis. One of the primary purposes of the groups is to pray for all the needs of all priests the world over. A particularized intention of the groups is to pray for the spiritual success of this newsletter.

The movement offers a spiritual way of life for the members of the chapters.

The chapters are open to all—to all persons of all vocational states of life. A handbook which explains the movement, offers the spiritual way of life, and provides details for procedures at chapter meetings, is available upon request. You may obtain this by writing us at the address on the back page of the newsletter.

## NOTES

1. Scriptural quotations are taken from *The Jerusalem Bible*, Doubleday & Co.
2. Archbishop Joseph Bernardin, *Called To Serve, Called To Lead*, St. Anthony Messenger Press, pp. 17-20.
3. Henri Nouwen, *In the Name of Jesus*, pp. 31-32.
4. St. John Eudes, from a treatise on the Admirable Heart of Jesus, as in *The Liturgy of the Hours*, Catholic Book Publishing Co., Vol. IV, pp. 1331-32.
5. Karl Rahner, S.J., *Spiritual Exercises*, Herder & Herder, pp. 117-118.
6. St. Teresa of Avila, *Interior Castle*, translated by E. Allison Peers, Doubleday & Co., "Second Mansions", p. 51.
7. Ibid., "Fourth Mansions", p. 76.
8. John Powell, S.J., *The Christian Vision*, Argus Communications, p. 147.
9. Arthur Collins, *Totus Tuus: John Paul's Program of Marian Consecration and Entrustment*, Academy of the Immaculata, p. 177.
10. St. Louis de Montfort, *God Alone: The Collected Writings of St. Louis de Montfort*, Montfort Publications, p. 327.

A Publication of
Shepherds of Christ
Ministries

# shepherds of Christ

## A SPIRITUALITY NEWSLETTER FOR PRIESTS

NOVEMBER/ DECEMBER 1994

# Chief Shepherd of the Flock

"I am the Good Shepherd: the Good Shepherd is one who lays down His life for His sheep. The hired man, since he is not the shepherd and the sheep do not belong to him, abandons the sheep and runs away as soon as he sees a wolf coming, and then the wolf attacks and scatters the sheep. This is because he is only a hired man and has no concern for the sheep. I am the Good Shepherd. I know My own and My own know Me, just as the Father knows Me and I know the Father. And I lay down My life for My sheep." (Jn 10: 11-15[1]).

Yes, the Good Shepherd has laid down His life for His sheep. The Good Shepherd's magnificent Heart, overflowing with love for His Father and all of us, was pierced so that the waters of our salvation might flow forth: "It was Preparation Day, and to prevent the bodies remaining on the cross during the sabbath—since that sabbath was a day of special solemnity—the Jews asked Pilate to have the legs broken and the bodies taken away. Consequently the soldiers came and broke the legs of the first man who had been crucified with him and then of the other. When they came to Jesus, they found he was already dead, and so instead of breaking his legs one of the soldiers pierced his side with a lance. And immediately there came out blood and water." (Jn 19: 31-34).

Bonaventure, the Franciscan saint and doctor of the Church, comments on the pierced Heart of the Good Shepherd: "Then, in order that the Church might be formed out of the side of Christ sleeping on the cross...the divine plan permitted that one of the soldiers pierce open His sacred side with a lance. While blood mixed with water flowed, the price of our salvation was poured forth, which gushing forth from the sacred fountain of the heart gave power to the sacraments of the Church..."[2]

Another doctor of the Church, St. Augustine, also refers to the source of life which is the pierced Heart of Jesus: "On the cross he made a great exchange. The purse which held our price was opened, for when the soldier's spear opened his side, the price of the whole world flowed forth."[3]

See *Chief Shepherd,* page 18, bottom

# Editor's Corner
by Edward Carter S.J.

We wish all our priest-readers a most happy and blessed New Year. During this coming year and always may God give us all abundant graces for our own spiritual growth and for the fruitfulness of our priestly ministry.

The feast of Christmas, which we have just celebrated, is an excellent time to remind ourselves of the reason for the Incarnation: "Yes, God loved the world so much that he gave his only Son, so that everyone who believes in him may not be lost but may have eternal life." (Jn 3: 16).

This brief scriptural passage in its own way summarizes the religion Christ came to give us. The passage in effect tells us that we are to be aware of God's love lavishly given to us in Jesus Christ, and that we are to respond with a love of our own, that we are to believe in Jesus Christ. We know, of course, that the biblical concept of faith includes the entire person, including the act of love whereby a person gives oneself to the following of Jesus. To repeat, the above passage from John's Gospel summarizes Christian existence: the awareness of God's love for us in Christ and our response of love in Christ—our love of God and neighbor.

A number of entries in this issue contain ideas regarding devotion to the Heart of Christ. I mention this consequent to what I have just said because devotion to the Heart of Christ gives us the same summary of Christian existence as does the above passage from John. Pius XII has left us these words: "...we readily understand that devotion to...the Heart of Jesus is essentially devotion to the love with which God loved us through Jesus and is at the same time an enlivening of our love for God and man. Or, to put it in other words, this devotion is directed to God's love for us in order to adore Him, to thank Him and to spend our lives imitating Him."[5]

---

*Chief Shepherd* continued from page 17

Finally, we have the words of the Church herself concerning the pierced Heart of Jesus. In the preface for the Mass of the Sacred Heart we read in part: "Lifted high on the cross, Christ gave his life for us, so much did he love us. From his wounded side flowed blood and water, the fountain of sacramental life in the Church. To his open heart the Savior invites all...to draw water in joy from the springs of salvation."[4]

Yes, the Church reminds us that Jesus the Good Shepherd invites all to come to His open Heart, this Heart which symbolizes His love and calls for our love in return. The Church invites all to come to Jesus' pierced Heart in order to be clothed with the graces which the Heart of Jesus longs to give us in abundance. We priests have the privilege and responsibility to lead the members of Jesus' flock to the pierced Heart of Jesus in order that they may be showered with the graces which are necessary for their salvation and ongoing sanctification. As a good shepherd under Jesus, Chief Shepherd of the Flock, the priest has to lead the sheep to the only source of true nourishment, the pierced Heart of Christ. The more we priests ourselves dwell within the pierced Heart of Jesus, as the Church invites all to do, the more we are able to lead others to this sacred refuge and source of all spiritual nourishment. As we ourselves dwell within the pierced Heart of Jesus, Christ gives us an increased awareness of how much He loves each person with the most special and unique love. Jesus has chosen each priest to be a most special ambassador to spread the message of this overwhelming love of His Heart for each individual. The more we priests ourselves grow in the awareness of how much Jesus loves each of us as His priest-companions, the more we are able to teach to others the truth of Jesus' special love for each individual. And the more we priests realize how much Jesus wants the love of each individual, the more we are also able to teach His truth to others.

Jesus suffered and died for the entire human race, but He did it in a manner which makes it true to say He also did it for each individual in a most special way. Notice how personalized St. Paul makes the redemptive suffering and death and love of Jesus. In the letter to the Galatians he does not use the plural, but the singular: "I have been crucified with Christ, and the life I live now is not my own; Christ is living in me. I still live my human life, but it is a life of faith in the Son of God, who loved me and gave himself for me." (Gal 2: 19-20).

# The Eucharist: Source and Summit of Christian Life

Our personal relationship with Christ is characterized by the realization of the great, special love of His Heart for each of us and of our need to love Him in return. The chief source for growth in this personal relationship with Jesus is the Eucharist. The New Catechism tells us: "The Eucharist is 'the source and summit of the Christian life.' The other sacraments, and indeed all ecclesiastical mysteries and work of the apostolate, are bound up with the Eucharist and are oriented toward it. For in the blessed Eucharist is contained the whole spiritual good of the Church, namely Christ himself, our Pasch."[6]

# Pope John Paul II, St. John Vianney and The Heart of Christ

Pope John Paul II reminds us of the key role devotion to the Heart of Jesus played in the life of the inspirational priest-saint, John Vianney, the Cure of Ars: "The Cure of Ars is a model of priestly zeal for all pastors. The secret of his generosity is to be found without doubt in his *love of God,* lived without limits, in constant response to the love made manifest *in Christ crucified.* This is where he bases his desire to do everything to save the souls ransomed by Christ at such a great price, and to bring them back to the love of God. Let us recall one of those pithy sayings which he had the knack of uttering: 'The priesthood is the love of the Heart of Jesus.' In his sermons and catechesis he continually returned to that love: 'O my God, I prefer to die loving you than to live a single instant without loving you...'

"Dear brother priests, nourished by the Second Vatican Council which has felicitously placed the priest's consecration within the framework of his pastoral mission, let us join Saint John Vianney and seek the dynamism of our pastoral zeal in the Heart of Jesus, in his love for souls. If we do not draw from the same source, our ministry risks bearing little fruit."[7]

# Henri Nouwen on the Need for Theological Reflection

Henri Nouwen, one of the most influential writers of our times, also refers to the Heart of Christ in these provocative words on theological reflection: "Few ministers and priests think theologically. Most of them have been educated in a climate in which the behavioral sciences, such as psychology and sociology, so dominated the educational milieu that little true theology was being learned. Most Christian leaders today raise psychological or sociological questions even though they frame them in scriptural terms. Real, theological thinking, which is thinking with the mind of Christ, is hard to find in the practice of the ministry. Without solid theological reflection, future leaders will be little more than pseudo-psychologists, pseudo-sociologists, pseudo-social workers...

"The task of future Christian leaders is not to make a little contribution to the solution of the pain and tribulations of their time, but to identify and announce the ways in which Jesus is leading God's people out of slavery, through the desert to a new land of freedom...In short, they have to say 'no' to the secular world and proclaim in unambiguous terms that the incarnation of God's Word, through whom all things came into being, has made even the smallest event of human history into Kairos, that is, *an opportunity to be led deeper into the heart of Christ...* (emphasis that of the editor).

"Thinking about the future of Christian leadership, I am convinced that it needs to be a theological leadership. For this to come about, much—very much—has to happen in seminaries and divinity schools. They have to become centers where people are trained in true discernment of the signs of the time. This cannot be just an intellectual training. It requires a deep spiritual formation involving the whole person—body, mind, and heart. I think we are only half aware of how secular even theological schools have become. Formation in the mind of Christ, who did not cling to power but emptied himself, taking the form of a slave, is not what most seminaries are about. Everything in our competitive and ambitious world militates against it. But to the degree that such formation is being sought for and realized, there is hope for the Church of the next century."[8]

# Promises of Our Lord & Rahner's Commentary

The following promises of Our Lord were given to St. Margaret Mary Alacoque regarding those who are devoted to His Heart. Following the promises is Karl Rahner's commentary on the same.

1. I will give them all the graces necessary in their state of life.
2. I will establish peace in their homes.
3. I will comfort them in all their afflictions.
4. I will be their secure refuge during life, and above all in death.
5. I will bestow abundant blessings. upon all their undertakings.
6. Sinners shall find in My Heart the source and infinite ocean of mercy.
7. Lukewarm souls shall become fervent.
8. Fervent souls shall quickly mount to high perfection.
9. I will bless every place in which an image of My Heart is exposed and honored.
10. I will give to priests the gift of touching the most hardened hearts.
11. Those who promote this devotion shall have their names written in My Heart, never to be blotted out.
12. I promise you in the excessive mercy of My Heart that My all-powerful love will grant to all those who receive Holy Communion on the First Fridays in nine consecutive months the grace of final penitence; they shall not die in My disgrace, nor without receiving their Sacraments. My Divine Heart shall be their refuge.[9]

Here is Rahner's commentary regarding these promises: "Taken in their entirety, these promises affirm and offer no more than our Lord promised in the Gospel to absolute faith…What is new in these promises is therefore not their content, but the circumstances of their fulfillment, the fact that what has already been promised in substance in the Gospels is now attached precisely to devotion to the Sacred Heart. To anyone with a grasp of the devotion, who practices it in the deep unconditional faith that it demands, this 'new' element in the promises will offer no special problem."[10]

# Act of Consecration

Lord Jesus, Chief Shepherd of the Flock, I consecrate my priestly life to Your Heart, pierced on Calvary for love of us. From Your pierced Heart the Church was born, the Church You have called me, as a priest, to serve in a most special way. You reveal Your Heart as symbol of Your love in all its aspects, including Your most special love for me, whom You have chosen as Your priest-companion. Help me always to pour out my life in love of God and neighbor. Heart of Jesus, I place my trust in You!

Dear Blessed Virgin Mary, I consecrate myself to your maternal and Immaculate Heart, this Heart which is symbol of your life and love. You are the Mother of my Savior. You are also my Mother. You love me with the most special love as this unique priest-son. In return of love I give myself entirely to your motherly love and protection. You followed Jesus perfectly. You are His first and perfect disciple. Teach me to imitate you in the putting on of Christ. Be my motherly intercessor so that, through your Immaculate Heart, I may be guided to an ever closer union with the pierced Heart of Jesus, Chief Shepherd of the Flock, who leads me to the Father in the Holy Spirit.

# Vatican II on Priestly Holiness

Living out our life of consecration is living the life of holiness. Vatican II speaks to us about the priestly life of holiness: "By the sacrament of orders priests are configured to Christ the Priest so that as ministers of the Head and co-workers of the episcopal order they can build up and establish His whole Body which is the Church. Already, indeed, in the consecration of baptism, like all Christians, they received the sign and the gift of so lofty a vocation and a grace that even despite human weakness they can and must pursue according to the Lord's words: 'You therefore are to be perfect, even as your heavenly Father is perfect' (Mt 5:48).

"To the acquisition of this perfection priests are bound by a special claim, since they have been consecrated to God in a new way by the reception of orders. They have become living instruments of Christ the eternal priest, so that through the ages they can accomplish His wonderful work of reuniting the whole society of men with heavenly power. Therefore, since every priest in his own way represents Christ Himself, he is also enriched with special grace...

"Priestly holiness itself contributes very greatly to a fruitful fulfillment of the priestly ministry. True, the grace of God can complete the work of salvation even through unworthy ministers. Yet ordinarily God desires to manifest His works through those who have been made particularly docile to the impulse and guidance of the Holy Spirit. Because of their intimate union with Christ and their holiness of life, these men can say with the Apostle: 'It is now no longer I that live, but Christ lives in me' (Gal 2:20)"[11].

# St. Charles Borromeo On The Necessity of Prayer

One of the most necessary means for growth in the life of holiness of which Vatican II speaks is prayer. St. Charles Borromeo speaks to priests about this: "We must meditate before, during and after everything we do. The prophet says, *'I will pray, and then I will understand.'* When you administer the sacraments, meditate on what you are doing. When you celebrate Mass, reflect on the sacrifice you are offering. When you pray the office, think about the words you are saying and the Lord to whom you are speaking. When you take care of your people, meditate on the Lord's blood that has washed them clean. In this way, *all that you do becomes a work of love.*

"This is the way we can easily overcome the countless difficulties we have to face day after day, which, after all, are part of our work: in meditation we find the strength to bring Christ to birth in ourselves and in other men."[12]

# The New Catechism and Social Justice

Our life of holiness must have a social dimension. The more we go to the Father, through Christ, in the Holy Spirit, with Mary our Mother at our side, the more we grow in concern for others. One aspect of our concern for others is our work in promoting social justice. The new Catechism reminds us of truths upon which social justice must be based: "Social justice can be obtained only in respecting the transcendent dignity of man...

"Respect for the human person entails respect for the rights that flow from his dignity as a creature...

"Respect for the human person proceeds by way of respect for the principle that everyone should look upon his neighbor (without any exception) as 'another self', above all bearing in mind his life and the means necessary for living it with dignity. No legislation could by itself do away with the fears, prejudices, and attitudes of pride and selfishness which obstruct the establishment of truly fraternal societies. Such behavior will cease only through the charity that finds in every man 'a neighbor', a brother.

"The duty of making oneself a neighbor to others and actively serving them becomes even more urgent when it involves the disadvantaged, in whatever area this may be. 'As you did it to one of the least of these my brethren, you did it to me.'

"The same duty extends to those who think or act differently from us. The teaching of Christ goes so far as to require forgiveness of offenses. He extends the commandment of love, which is that of the New Law, to all enemies. Liberation in the spirit of the Gospel is incompatible with hatred of one's enemy as a person, but not with hatred of the evil that he does as an enemy."[13]

## NOTES

1. Scriptural quotations are taken from *The Jerusalem Bible,* Doubleday & Co.
2. Bonaventure, tr. by E. Cousins, Paulist Press, pp. 154-155.
3. The Liturgy of the Hours, Catholic Book Publishing Co., Vol. IV, 1727.
4. The Sacramentary, Catholic Book Publishing Co., p. 463.
5. Pius XII, Haurietis Aquas, Catholic Mind, (1956), Part IV.
6. The Catechism of the Catholic Church, p. 397.
7. Letter of Pope John Paul II to All Priests of the Church for Holy Thursday 1986, St. Paul Editions.
8. Henri Nouwen, *In the Name of Jesus,* Crossword Pub., pp. 65-70.
9. Alban Dachauer, S.J., The Sacred Heart, Bruce Pub., pp. 147-148.
10. Karl Rahner, S.J., as in The Heart of the Redeemer, Trinity Communications, p. 140.
11. The Documents of Vatican II, Decree on the Ministry and Life of Priests, America Press Edition,
    Ch. 3, No. 12.
12. The Liturgy of the Hours, op. cit., Vol.. IV, p. 1727.
13. The Catechism of the Catholic Church, op. cit., p. 460.

A Publication of
Shepherds of Christ
Ministries

# shepherds of Christ

## A SPIRITUALITY NEWSLETTER FOR PRIESTS

JANUARY/FEBRUARY 1995

# Chief Shepherd of the Flock

"I am the Good Shepherd: the Good Shepherd is one who lays down His life for His sheep. The hired man, since he is not the shepherd and the sheep do not belong to him, abandons the sheep and runs away as soon as he sees a wolf coming, and then the wolf attacks and scatters the sheep. This is because he is only a hired man and has no concern for the sheep. I am the Good Shepherd. I know My own and My own know Me, just as the Father knows Me and I know the Father. And I lay down My life for My sheep." (Jn 10: 11-15[1]).

Yes, out of His great love for us, the Good Shepherd laid down His life for us. Love for His Father and for us led the Good Shepherd to the brutal death on the cross. The Incarnation is, indeed, centered in love. Our insight into the Christ-event deepens as we consider it in the light of love. The Father has given us a sign of His love for us in Jesus. Jesus Himself is this sign of the Father's love—a lavish sign, an unmistakable sign, an irrevocable sign, a perfect sign. We are meant, then, to understand the meaning of the Son's becoming man in terms of love. We are to draw from the riches contained in the Christ-event in terms of love. We live Jesus, we live the Christ-event, in proportion to our acceptance of God's love and our own return of love. As we grow in love of God and neighbor, we give greater witness to the Incarnation, which is a work of God's love. Jesus reveals His Heart to remind us of all this. His pierced Heart, symbol of God's overwhelming love for us, calls for our love of God and neighbor in return.

# Reflections on Love

The above thoughts give us an occasion to offer various reflections on love:

◆ He was consistently motivated by love. In the end He was literally consumed by love, for it led Him to a place called Calvary. He was brutally nailed to a cross and raised up midst the laughter and ridicule of enemies.

See *Chief Shepherd,* page 26, bottom

25

# Editor's Corner
by Edward Carter S.J.

The New Year, with its connotations of newness, is an occasion to remind ourselves that Christ has come to give us newness of life. Indeed, in Christ, we are new creatures: "And for anyone who is in Christ, there is a new creation; the old creation has gone, and now the new one is here." (2Cor 5:17).

As we begin the New Year, we have an appropriate opportunity to resolve to live this newness of life Jesus has given us at a deeper level. Another way of putting this is to say that the inception of the New Year gives us an opportunity to resolve to avoid spiritual mediocrity. Let's resolve to live each day of the New Year—and all the days of the rest of our lives—at the deepest spiritual level possible. Jesus comes to us anew each day with the invitation to enter into His life ever more deeply. Let's resolve not to waste these daily invitations of Our Lord. If we respond each day to Jesus' call to come closer to Him that day, we will avoid spiritual mediocrity. We will be gradually opening ourselves more and more to the immense, personal love which Jesus has for each one of us. We will be giving ourselves to Christ with an ever greater love. We will be experiencing peace and joy in ever greater measure—for peace and joy are the two chief fruits of love.

---

*Chief Shepherd* continued from page 25

He hung there, bruised and beaten, His body smeared with blood. There was the flush of fever mixed with the chill of approaching death. The greatest physical suffering was surpassed only by an unfathomable anguish of spirit. It was a terrible scene, yet one permeated with a haunting beauty which came forth from the magnificent love of His Heart. His crucified figure, silhouetted against a darkening sky, is the everlasting reminder that to live is to love, and that to love involves not only joy, but also suffering.

♦ We are great because of what we are, and we are to the extent that we love God and neighbor.

♦ Love is sensitive. It is delicately aware of the loved one's needs. Moreover, love's sensitivity is blended with a strength and durability which allows it to endure pain, hardship, and difficulty for the beloved.

♦ Love is sensitive, not only regarding those few especially loved in close personal relationships. Love is sensitive also regarding all others, especially the poor and underprivileged and those whom the world passes by as unimportant, the sick and the lame also, and likewise all those who seem especially weighed down by the burden of life.

◆ When love fails, it does not remain mired in discouragement. It resolves to learn from past mistakes and henceforth to love more selflessly, more deeply, more tenderly.

◆ Why are we sometimes afraid of God's love? We shy away from the white heat of His love, foolishly thinking He will ask too much of us. When has He ever asked for something too difficult? When has He ever asked anything without giving us abundant grace to accomplish His desire? When has His love ever asked that which has not brought us closer to Him, thus enhancing our happiness?

◆ Jesus loves us with an overwhelming love. Why do we at times find it difficult to love ourselves? Jesus sees our failings, but also all the good we do with the help of His grace. He also sees our capacity for achieving ever greater good. Why do we at times become depressed at what we are not, rather than being encouraged at what God has helped us to be?

◆ A number of years ago an educator wrote the following. Perhaps what he said then is even more applicable today: "I could not even begin to count the men and women whom I have met in my work who testify, with great sadness, that their formation/education both at home and at school was almost completely in terms of achievement, of doing, of performing according to standards, of accomplishing certain narrow goals, but hardly ever in terms of being, of growing, of loving."[2]

◆ When loving God and neighbor becomes difficult and painful, there is a temptation to turn in a non-love direction which deceptively appears to be free of pain and suffering. Pursuing such a path, however, is a dead-end street where one painfully suffocates in selfish self-enclosement.

◆ Although love must be firm when necessary, it is also gentle. Love does not further crush the bruised personality, but helps the other to heal and grow through tenderness and affirmation.

◆ Love can cause one to weep. Sometimes the tears are caused by joy, at other times by pain.

◆ Love helps a person to be enthusiastic about life, sometimes ecstatically so, more often quietly so.

◆ Jesus has told us to focus on love. Is it not strange that we Christians, who call ourselves His followers, can at times so easily allow other concerns to dominate our consciousness?

◆ The bloated stomachs of starving children, the tragedies of broken homes, the rat-infected ghettoes, the drug scene with its dreadful number of ruined lives, city streets engraved with an alarmingly increasing list of murders, rapes, and muggings—when love sees all of this, it weeps. Love not only weeps, however. It also acts.

◆ "If I have all the eloquence of men or of angels, but speak without love,

I am simply a gong booming or a cymbal clashing. If I have the gift of prophecy, understanding all the mysteries there are, and knowing everything, and if I have faith in all its fullness, to move mountains, but without love, then I am nothing at all. If I give away all that I possess, piece by piece, and if I even let them take my body to burn it, but am without love, it will do me no good whatever" (1 Cor 13: 1-3).

# The Priest and Friendship

One of the ways all of us experience love—both giving and receiving love—is through friendship. The *Directory on the Ministry and Life of Priests* offers some thoughts on the priest and friendship: "The capacity to develop and profoundly live priestly friendship is a source of serenity and joy in the exercise of the ministry, a decisive support in difficulties and a valuable help in the growth of pastoral charity. Priests must exercise this friendship in a particular way precisely towards those brothers most in need of understanding, help and support."[3]

Friendship is one of God's greatest gifts. It is a type of personal relationship that befits any age and any vocation. One of the beauties of friendship is the special type of love that is involved. Two people become friends and remain friends because they mutually want to do so. In friendship, there are no juridical bonds as there are in marriage and family life. In real friendship, this special freedom that both parties possess regarding the initiation and maintenance of the relationship does not instigate insecure feelings, but rather enhances the relationship with a special kind of splendor.

One of the beauties of friendship is the obvious fact that a person may have more than one friend. A person should not view multiple friendships as being in competition with one another. A person's various authentic friendships, all providing their own opportunities for growth, clothe the person with a maturing richness of personality that increasingly contributes to the health of each of the friendships in particular.

Close friends stand side by side and together walk the path of life. Secure in each other's acceptance and love, each feels a sense of relief that one does not need to maintain any kind of facade. Each is encouraged to be and to become according to the real, true self. Far from hampering the proper unfolding and developing of each one's personality, the friendship offers many diverse opportunities for the maturing of each other's uniqueness. Indeed, each person feels that without the other he or she may not have grown in certain ways at all.

Close friends share many things. They share life's ideals and goals, for example, and in this sharing feel encouraged to achieve a greater realization of these ideals and goals. Close friends share each other's sorrows, and in this sharing the sorrows become more bearable. Close friends share each other's failures, and in this sharing they gain the strength to rise and try again. Close friends also share each other's successes, and in this sharing are encouraged to fulfill more and more their mission, their work in life.

Each of us, then, has many reasons to thank God for the wonderful gift of friendship, for, indeed, friendship in so many diverse ways has helped us to be and to become. In so many diverse ways, the gift if friendship has helped us to live the paschal mystery of death and resurrection. Truly, it has helped us bear the dark, the difficult, the worrisome aspect of life with greater equanimity. Likewise, it has helped us experience the bright, the pleasant, the exuberant side of life with greater joy.

We should always remember that all of our friendships should be rooted in Christ. To put it another way, our very friendship with Jesus is the source for our ability to be true friends with others. And, of course, our friendship with Jesus is centered in love. This friend Jesus shows each of us His Heart as a reminder of how much He loves each one of us with the most unique and special love. And He longs for our love in return. What a privilege! Yes, what a privilege it is to be invited by the Incarnate Son of God to have the deepest friendship with Himself. Jesus has left us these beautiful and awe-inspiring words: "I shall not call you servants any more, because a servant does not know his master's business; I call you friends, because I have made known to you everything I have learned from My Father." (Jn 15:15).

# Pope John Paul II on Faithfulness

The Holy Father offers us some very meaningful words on the subject of faithfulness. Faithfulness, of course, is one of the chief characteristics of love: "Virgo fidelis, the faithful Virgin. What does this faithfulness of Mary mean? What are the dimensions of this faithfulness? The first dimension is called search. Mary was faithful first of all when she began, lovingly, to seek the deep sense of God's plan in her and for the world. 'Quomodo fiet? How shall this be?', she asked the Angel of the Annunciation.

"The second dimension of faithfulness is called reception, acceptance. The quomodo fiet is changed, on Mary's lips, to a fiat, 'Let it be done, I am ready, I accept.' This is the moment in which man perceives that he will never completely understand the 'how'; that there are in God's plan more areas of mystery than of clarity; that, however he may try, he will never succeed in understanding it completely...

"The third dimension of faithfulness is consistency to live in accordance with what one believes; to adapt one's life to the object of one's adherence. To accept misunderstanding, persecutions, rather than a break between what one practices and what one believes; this is consistency...

"But all faithfulness must pass the most exacting test, that of duration. Therefore, the fourth dimension of faithfulness is constancy. It is easy to be consistent for a day or two. It is difficult and important to be consistent for one's whole life. It is easy to be consistent in the hour of enthusiasm. It is difficult to be so in the hour of tribulation."[4]

# The Source of Our Faithfulness

It is impossible to incorporate into our lives the dimensions of faithfulness about which the Pope speaks without a meaningful and evolving union with Jesus. Mary was Jesus' most faithful follower because she had the greatest, the deepest love-union with Him.

Our love-union with Jesus is centered in our Eucharistic devotion, The more we take the means to draw from the infinite source of grace which is the pierced, Eucharistic Heart of Jesus, the more we are united with Him, and, consequently, the more one's faithfulness grows. Our union with the Eucharistic Christ, in turn, depends greatly on our spirit of prayer. A consistent prayer life is necessary for the proper assimilation of the graces which flow from the Eucharist. Here, then, are our great means for our growth in union with Jesus: the Eucharist and prayer. And, again, increased union with Jesus means increased faithfulness. Let us ask Mary, the faithful Virgin, and our faithful Mother, to obtain for us the grace to grow in our appreciation of the Eucharist and the life of prayer. If we grow in this appreciation, and live accordingly, we come ever closer to Jesus, who desires to lead us to an ever deeper union with the Father in the Holy Spirit.

Some of the above thoughts are contained in the following passage from the *Directory on the Ministry and Life of Priests:*

"To remain faithful to the obligation of 'being with Christ', it is necessary that the priest know how to imitate the Church in prayer...

"Strengthened by the special bond with the Lord the priest will know how to confront those moments in which he could feel alone among men; effectively renewing his being with Christ who in the Eucharist is his refuge and best repose.

"Like Christ, who was often alone with the Father (cf Lk 3:21; Mk 1:35), the priest also must be the man who finds communion with God in solitude, so he can say with St. Ambrose: 'I am never less alone than as when I am alone…"[5]

# Merton on Prayer

I think it is safe to say that no spiritual writer of our times has written more prolifically on prayer than has Thomas Merton. His following words help us to continue what has been said above concerning the importance of prayer:

"Meditation is a twofold discipline that has a twofold function. First it is supposed to give you sufficient control over your mind and memory and will to enable you to recollect yourself and withdraw from exterior things and the business and activities and thoughts and concerns of temporal existence, and second—this is the real end of meditation—it teaches you how to become aware of the presence of God; and most of all it aims at bringing you to a state of almost constant loving attention to God and dependence on Him."[6]

# Making the Most of Life's Opportunities

Love—together with its faithfulness—bids us to make the most of life's opportunities. Fr. Philip Hamilton, currently a pastor and formerly an Air Force chaplain and college professor, encourages us to seize the God-given opportunities for contributing to the life of God's kingdom:

"Tucked away on the back pages of most of the Catholic newspapers that I read was an article about a great man's death. The man has certainly been one of the most influential priests in the history of our country. He was Father Patrick Peyton.

"Father Peyton was born in County Mayo in Ireland. He came to the United States in 1928 with his brother Thomas. The two brothers entered the seminary joining the priests at Notre Dame in the Society of the Holy Cross. As a seminarian he contracted tuberculosis. He prayed to our Blessed Mother that he might be cured and be able to be ordained a priest. He was, and lived to the age of eighty-three…

"Father Peyton, Irish immigrant that he was, moved hundreds of thousands, perhaps millions, to a renewed appreciation of the rosary. He is said to be the author of the phrase, 'the family that prays together stays together'. And the rosary was the prayer that he offered the family. He traveled the world preaching the rosary. People came by the thousands.

"Father had a dream as a young priest. His faith and optimism made that dream a reality. How many young priests, perhaps much more talented than he, had such a dream? Perhaps even I. Yet instead of lacking confidence in self and others, he boldly went forward and with the grace of God deeply affected the lives of millions while the rest of us, in our cautionary security, continued in our little ways free of fear because we never tried. We were always satisfied with small success. How many thousands of young men and women, probably dozens even on Hilton Head, could touch people as Father Peyton; but they never will because they have become satisfied with the living without fear or rejection through not having tried.

"I am seventy-four years old; but as I think of Father Peyton while writing this little essay at five a.m. here in my office, I am filled with the eagerness in the years left me to shout loud and publicly, 'Look out world, here I come to bring you the Good News of Christ! You and your children are going to know that I have been here telling you, showing you Who Christ is and what He can do in your lives.'

"That is how thinking about a man like Father Peyton affects me. What does he do for you?"[7]

# Mary and the Priest

Our friendship with Jesus as His priest-companions, our faithfulness to Him because we love Him, very much involves Mary. She, under God, is the Mother of our Christ-life. She cooperates with the Holy Spirit in our ongoing transformation in Christ. Fr. Arthur Calkins, a contemporary Marian scholar, offers us these words on Mary and the priest:

"If every Christian ought to see himself in the Apostle John, entrusted to Mary as her son or daughter, how much more ought priests to recognize themselves as sons of Mary, as the subjects of a 'double' entrustment to her. I say 'double', because they are successors of John by a twofold title: as disciples and as priests. This is beautifully drawn out by our Holy Father in his *Holy Thursday Letter to Priests* of 1988: 'If John at the foot of the Cross somehow represents every man and woman for whom the motherhood of the Mother of God is spiritually extended, how much more does this concern each of us , who are sacramentally called to the priestly ministry of the Eucharist in the Church!'

"No doubt there are any number of priests today who would say that such reasoning represents a certain 'snob appeal', a 'clerical culture' that should have disappeared after the Council. The emphasis now, they would maintain, is on equality: we all share the common priesthood of the faithful and priestly ordination does not make us better than lay people.

"Surely, it is true that the hierarchical priesthood which is received by the imposition of the bishop's hands is conferred on the basis of the royal priesthood which all the faithful share. It is also true that of itself priestly ordination does not make one morally better than the laity...

"But the fact is that the Sacrament of Holy Orders configures the priest more closely to Christ the Eternal Priest to the extent that his soul receives an indelible spiritual character and his very being is transformed in a way that

allows him to function *in persona Christi*, in the very person of Christ, as he celebrates the sacraments and intercedes as a member of and on behalf of the whole Church. Hence this scriptural injunction surely holds true for the priest: 'When much has been given a man, much will be required of him. More will be asked of a man to whom more has been entrusted' (Lk 12:48). Saint Thomas Aquinas puts it this way: 'Those who have been chosen for a superior position through the bestowal of Holy Orders also have been called to a similar height of holiness' (Summa Theologica, suppl., q. 35, a. 1, ad 3)...

"Although Jesus had already entrusted every priest to his Mother from the height of the cross and the Pope has done it even hundreds of times, it is still necessary for the priest to do so himself if he would truly experience the power and the protection of the Mother of God in his life as her Divine Son intends it. Priests who have done so know the difference it makes.[8]

# Act of Consecration

Lord Jesus, Chief Shepherd of the Flock, I consecrate my priestly life to Your Heart, pierced on Calvary for love of us. From Your pierced Heart the Church was born, the Church You have called me, as a priest, to serve in a most special way. You reveal Your Heart as symbol of Your love in all its aspects, including Your most special love for me, whom You have chosen as Your priest-companion. Help me always to pour out my life in love of God and neighbor. Heart of Jesus, I place my trust in You!

Dear Blessed Virgin Mary, I consecrate myself to your maternal and Immaculate Heart, this Heart which is symbol of your life and love. You are the Mother of my Savior. You are also my Mother. You love me with the most special love as this unique priest-son. In a return of love I give myself entirely to your motherly love and protection. You followed Jesus perfectly. You are His first and perfect disciple. Teach me to imitate you in the putting on of Christ. Be my motherly intercessor so that, through your Immaculate Heart, I may be guided to an ever closer union with the pierced Heart of

Jesus, Chief Shepherd of the Flock, who leads me to the Father in the Holy Spirit.

# The Holy Spirit in Our Lives

As the closing words of the act of consecration remind us, Jesus leads us to the Father in the Holy Spirit. The Holy Spirit is given to us to transform us more and more according to the likeness of Christ. Mary our Mother cooperates with the Spirit, Whose spouse she is, in this process. Obviously, we should pray to the Holy Spirit each day. Here is one of the available prayers: "Come, Holy Spirit, almighty Sanctifier. God of love, Who filled the Virgin Mary with grace, Who wonderfully changed the hearts of the apostles, Who endowed all your martyrs with miraculous courage, come and sanctify us. Enlighten our minds, strengthen our wills, purify our consciences, rectify our judgment, set our hearts on fire, and preserve us from the misfortunes of resisting Your inspirations. Amen."

# St. Therese and the Heart of Christ

The following words of St. Therese of Lisieux, contained in a letter to one of her sisters, have an obvious connection with the above act of consecration to the Heart of Christ: "I myself find it very easy to practice perfection, for I know that all one has to do is to take Jesus by His Heart. Even if I had on my conscience every sin it is possible to commit, I should fling myself, my heart broken with sorrow, into the arms of Jesus, for I know He loves the prodigal child who returns to Him."[9]

# Letters

We wish to thank most sincerely all those who have taken the time to write us letters. Because of rather stringent space limitations, we can print only a very few of these. The ones we print are, for the most part, picked at random.

I read with deep interest your edition of *Shepherds of Christ*. It is spiritually based, neatly organized, and very readable. Again, congratulations on a beautiful ministry.

Rev. Joseph F. Brennan
Pastor, St. Genevieve Church
LaFayette, Louisiana

Thank you for sending me the newsletter, *Shepherds of Christ.* I loved it. I need all the help you can give during these confusing times. I must not lose sight of my objective—a true salesman for Our Lord. I must be sold first to love Him before I bring others to Him.

Fr. Sabbas R.
Christ the King Rectory
Commack, L.I., New York

# Apostleship of Prayer Anniversary

December 3, 1994, marked the 150th anniversary of the Apostleship of Prayer. The Apostleship has done much over the years to promote devotion to the Heart of Jesus and to the Heart of Mary within the context of the Morning Offering.

NOTES:

1. Scriptural quotations are taken from *The Jerusalem Bible,* Doubleday & Company.
2. Michael Lawrence, C.SS.P., *You Have to Love to Teach,* Ligourian, September 1974, p.4.
3. *Directory on the Ministry and Life of Priests,* as in special supplement of *Inside the Vatican,* p. 11.
4. Pope John Paul II, *Inside the Vatican,* December, 1994, pp. 29-39.
5. *Directory on the Ministry and Life of Priests,* op. cit., p.15.
6. Thomas Merton, *Seeds of Contemplation,* Dell Books, p.129.
7. Fr. Philip Hamilton, *Padre's Point,* Alt Pub. Co., pp. 151-152.
8. Fr. Arthur Calkins, *Soul Magazine,* January-February 1995, p. 30.
9. J. Beevers, *St. Therese, The Little Flower, The Making of a Saint,* Tan Publishers, p. 136.

A Publication of
Shepherds of Christ
Ministries

# shepherds of Christ

## A SPIRITUALITY NEWSLETTER FOR PRIESTS

MARCH/APRIL 1995

# Chief Shepherd of the Flock

"I am the Good Shepherd: the Good Shepherd is one who lays down His life for His sheep. The hired man, since he is not the shepherd and the sheep do not belong to him, abandons the sheep and runs away as soon as he sees a wolf coming, and then the wolf attacks and scatters the sheep. This is because he is only a hired man and has no concern for the sheep. I am the Good Shepherd. I know My own and My own know Me, just as the Father knows Me and I know the Father. And I lay down My life for My sheep." (Jn 10: 11-15[1]).

Indeed, the Good Shepherd has laid down His life for His sheep. During the recent events of Holy Week, we have called this truth to memory in a most special way. And on Easter, we have called to memory also in a most special fashion that the death of Jesus the Good Shepherd was for the purpose of life. In rising from the dead, Jesus achieved the life of resurrection, not only for Himself, but for us also.

The theme of death-resurrection is at the heart of Salvation history. In the Old Testament we see how the Jewish people, under the leadership of Moses, experienced death-resurrection as they were formed into the people of the covenant—Yahweh's people. In the great Exodus event they escaped Egyptian slavery, went on to Mt. Sinai where the covenant was ratified, and then progressed to the Promised Land. As members of the Mosaic covenant, as Yahweh's people, the Jews experienced a religious transition. They passed over to a higher level of religious existence, to a more intimate union with God.

This religious transition contained death-resurrection. For the Jews to become people of the covenant, to remain so, and to grow in the life of the covenant, it was necessary that they undergo a mystical or spiritual death. In short, the Jewish people had to be willing to pay a price; they had to be willing to bear with that which was difficult in covenant life. They had to be willing to die to that which was not according to God's will. This mystical death, however, had a very positive purpose. It was directed at life in the

See *Chief Shepherd,* page 38, bottom

# Editor's Corner
by Edward Carter S.J.

A number of our entries in this issue of the Newsletter deal explicitly with Christ's paschal mystery, with His death and resurrection. Since we have just celebrated the liturgies of Holy Week and Easter, we thought it a particularly apt time to present various ideas concerning the paschal mystery.

The reality of suffering has perennially been a problem for many. Some apparently are tempted to give up their religion when intense suffering enters their lives. They find it difficult to understand how the goodness of God would permit such suffering. There are others who become bitter because of suffering. Even though they once may have been the most attractive personalities, they become changed through their bitterness into persons who are burdens to themselves and others.

As is said elsewhere in this Newsletter, the real tragedy concerning suffering is not that there is so much of it. Rather the real tragedy is that so much of it seems to be wasted. When suffering is encountered according to God's will, it helps make a person more beautiful, more capable of love for God and neighbor, more apt for fulfilling one's unique role in life.

As priests we have numerous opportunities to help others suffer properly. The more we ourselves are united to the Christ Who suffered such a brutal death, the more we can help others see God's plan for suffering—that it is meant to lead to greater life:

"We had all gone astray like sheep, each taking his own way, and Yahweh burdened him with the sins of all of us. Harshly dealt with, he bore it humbly, he never opened his mouth, like a lamb that is led to the slaughterhouse, like a sheep that is dumb before its shearers never opening its mouth." (Is 53: 6-7).

---

*Chief Shepherd* continued from page 37

covenant and at growth in that life. This spiritual death, in other words, was aimed at resurrection.

Christ perfectly fulfilled the Old Testament theme of death and resurrection. In doing so He, too, was experiencing a religious transition. He was passing over—gradually, at first, and then definitively in His death—to a new kind of existence, to the life of His resurrection which He achieved not only for Himself, but for the entire human family. To achieve this new life of resurrection, Jesus was willing to pay the price. Jesus was willing to suffer, even unto a horrible death. That it had to be this way Jesus Himself pointed out to the two disciples on the road to Emmaus: "'You foolish men! So slow to believe the full message of the prophets! Was it not ordained that the Christ should suffer and so enter into His glory?' Then, starting with Moses and going through all the prophets, He explained to them the passages throughout the scriptures that were about Himself" (Lk 24: 25-27).

# St. Thomas Aquinas on the Sufferings of Christ

These thoughts of Thomas Aquinas easily follow from our previous considerations:

"Why did the Son of God have to suffer for us? There was a great need, and it can be considered in a twofold way: in the first place, as a remedy for sin, and secondly, as an example of how to act.

"It is a remedy, for in the face of all the evils of which we incur on account of our sins, we have found relief through the passion of Christ. Yet it is no less an example, for the passion of Christ completely suffices to fashion our lives. Whoever wishes to live perfectly should do nothing but disdain what Christ disdained on the cross and desire what he desired, for the cross exemplifies every virtue.

"If you seek the example of love: *Greater love than this no man has, than to lay down his life for his friends.* Such a man was Christ on the cross. And if he gave his life for us, then it should not be difficult to bear whatever hardships arise for his sake.

"If you seek patience, you will find no better example than the cross...Christ endured much on the cross, and did so patiently, because *when he suffered he did not threaten; he was led like a sheep to the slaughter and he did not open his mouth.* Therefore Christ's patience on the cross was great. *In patience let us run for the prize set before us, looking upon Jesus, the author and perfecter of our faith who, for the joy set before him, bore his cross and despised the shame.*

"If you seek an example of humility, look upon the crucified one, for God wished to be judged by Pontius Pilate and to die.

"If you seek an example of obedience, follow him who became obedient to the Father even unto death. *For just as by the disobedience of one man, namely, Adam, many were made sinners, so, by the obedience of one man, many were made righteous.*

"...follow him who is *the King and the Lord of lords, in whom are hidden all the treasures of wisdom and knowledge.* Upon the cross he was stripped, mocked, spat upon, struck, crowned with thorns, and given only vinegar and gall to drink.

"Do not be attached, therefore, to clothing and riches, because *they divided my garments among themselves.* Nor to honors, for he experienced harsh words and scourgings. Nor to greatness of rank, for *weaving a crown of thorns they placed it on my head.*"[2]

# On the Resurrected Christ

Here are words of Melito of Sardis, bishop, which, speaking of the Resurrected Christ, complement the previous words of Aquinas on the Suffering Christ:

"The Lord, though he was God, became man. He suffered for the sake of those who suffer, he was bound for those in bonds, condemned for the guilty, buried for those who lie in the grave; but he rose from the dead, and cried aloud: *Who will contend with me? Let him confront me.* I have freed the condemned, brought the dead back to life, raised men from their graves. Who has anything to say against me? I, he said, am the Christ; I have destroyed death, triumphed over the enemy, trampled hell underfoot, bound the strong one, and taken men up to the heights of heaven: I am the Christ.

"Come, then, all you nations of men, receive forgiveness for the sins that defile you. I am your forgiveness, I am the Passover that brings salvation. I am the lamb who was immolated for you. I am your ransom, your life, your resurrection, your light. I am your salvation and your king. I will bring you to the heights of heaven. With my own right hand I will raise you up, and I will show you the eternal Father."[3]

# St. Ambrose on the Paschal Mystery

These thoughts of St. Ambrose help us to continue our reflection on the Paschal Mystery:

"We have died with Christ. We carry about in our bodies the sign of his death, so that the living Christ may also be revealed in us. The life we live is not now our ordinary life but the life of Christ: a life of sinlessness, of chastity, of simplicity and every other virtue. We have risen with Christ. Let us live in Christ, let us ascend in Christ, so that the serpent may not have the power here below to wound us in the heel."[4]

# Our Participation in the Paschal Mystery

When we are baptized we are incorporated into Christ's paschal mystery of death and resurrection. St. Paul speaks of this marvelous assimilation to

Jesus: "You have been taught that when we were baptized in Christ Jesus we were baptized in his death; in other words, when we were baptized we went into the tomb with him and joined him in death, so that as Christ was raised from the dead by the Father's glory, we too might live a new life." (Rom 6: 3-4).

And, again: "...wherever we may be, we carry with us in our body the death of Jesus, so that the life of Jesus, too, may always be seen in our body." (2 Cor 4: 10-11).

Christ has structured the Christian life by the way He lived, died, and rose from the dead. It is obvious then, as Paul tells us above, that the pattern of death-resurrection must be at the heart of the Church's life. Individually and collectively, we continually die with Christ so that we may continually rise with Him. Thus we pass over in a process of continual religious transition to a greater participation in Jesus' resurrection. It is true that our participation in Christ's resurrection will reach its completion only in eternity. Nevertheless, we begin the life of resurrection here upon this earth, in the here and now of human life, in the midst of joy and pain, in the experience of success and failure, in the sweat of our brow, in the enjoyment of God's gifts. As Christians, we should have a sense of dynamic growth concerning our here-and-now life of resurrection.

We cannot maintain the life of resurrection or grow in it without a willingness to suffer. This does not mean that we need to feel overwhelmed and heavily burdened by the suffering in our lives. The greater portion of suffering for most Christians seems to be an accumulation of ordinary hardships, difficulties, and pains. At times, however, deep suffering, even suffering of agonizing proportions, can enter one's life. Whether the sufferings one encounters are of either the more ordinary variety or the more rare and extreme type, Christians must nevertheless convince themselves that to relate properly to the cross is to grow in resurrection, and for an individual to grow in resurrection means one will also have an increased capacity to help give resurrection to others.

# Reflections on Suffering

All of the above provides an occasion to offer various reflections on suffering:

◆ The great tragedy concerning human suffering is not that there is so much of it. The real tragedy is that apparently so much of it is wasted. So much of it apparently is not coped with according to God's will.

◆ Suffering can beautifully expand or bitterly constrict the personality. It is our choice which prevails.

◆ A willingness to suffer for a cause must accompany any true commitment.

- ◆ A persistent suffering is the necessity of bearing with our limitations.
- ◆ The fear of suffering is, for some people, one of the greatest crosses.
- ◆ True love, in any of its forms, must be experienced against the background of the cross. Jesus has very vividly shown us this. Strange, then, that at times we can strive to develop another pattern of loving.
- ◆ The suffering that is presently the most necessary for us is the one we can most consistently refuse.
- ◆ Happiness cannot be achieved without a proper encounter with suffering. This is a basic premise of the Christian message. It would seem, then, that we would eagerly embrace the cross. Yet how often is this the case?
- ◆ Being misunderstood by others precisely because we are striving to do God's will is a not uncommon suffering.
- ◆ To have to unavoidably hurt others can cause the sensitive person a suffering greater than the one he or she is inflicting.
- ◆ There is a part of us that does not want to surrender to God. This struggle between the true self and the false self produces a unique type of suffering which is persistently present, often in milder degrees, but occasionally with an intensity that pierces very suddenly and very sharply.
- ◆ It is not necessarily those who suffer the most who are the holiest. We grow in holiness through suffering—whatever its degree—to the extent we encounter it in loving conformity to God's will.
- ◆ The boredom that can grow out of daily routine, the frequent occasions which try one's patience, ordinary episodes of failure, minor annoyances of various kinds, anxieties—these and other forms of the daily cross do not, taken separately, require a Christian response of heroic proportions. But in their cumulative effect over a long period of time, such occasions offer us the opportunity of becoming love-inspired Christians to an eminent degree.
- ◆ There is nothing in the Christian teaching of the cross that says we cannot pray for relief from our sufferings.
- ◆ To want to flee suffering is an un-christian attitude. So also is the attempt to make suffering an end in itself. The Christ-event did not end on Calvary.
- ◆ "Then to all he said: 'If anyone wants to be a follower of mine, let him renounce himself and take up his cross every day and follow me.'" (Lk 9: 23).

# Reflections on Joy and Happiness

When we cope with suffering according to God's will, we grow in the Christ-life of grace. We grow in love. We grow in peace and joy. Suffering, which is properly encountered, consequently leads to a greater share in the joy of the resurrected Christ. There follow some reflections on joy:

◆ The Christian vocation includes the call to be joyful. If we live properly in Christ Jesus, we will increasingly share His resurrection joy despite the painful dimension of being human: "I have told you this so that my own joy may be in you and your joy be complete." (Jn 15:11).

◆ The Christian who is not fundamentally joyful presents a contradiction. He or she claims to be a follower of the Jesus who has promised abundant life, abundant joy. To remove the contradiction, such a Christian must look to himself or herself. Such a person does not lack a basic joy because there is anything wanting in Jesus' message. The person lacks joy because there is something wanting in the self. In some way or another, for some reason or another, the person has failed to assimilate properly the Gospel message. The Gospel is the good news. Jesus invites us to listen to His Gospel, to respond to it, to live it ever more fully and dynamically. Jesus tells us that if we do, we will experience a peace and joy that the world does not know. We know that Jesus does not lie, that Jesus does not deceive, that Jesus does not cruelly excite the expectations of His followers

and then fail to fulfill them. Again, if a Christian is lacking in joy, he or she has to look at the self and ask why. But one should not ask this question in isolation. One should ask it in the company of Jesus. Jesus will help the person find the answer. Jesus will help the person remedy the situation.

◆ Western, industrialized culture has tended to create the illusion that joy can be bought and that, the more money one has, the greater the prospects of enjoying life. This tragic illusion has time and again prevented people from living in a manner which alone can give true joy.

◆ Real and lasting joy comes only when we are consistently willing to expend the effort required to grow in union with Jesus. Since this effort is a graced effort—one accompanied by God's grace—we should pray daily for the grace to use the means God has put before us to grow in union with Jesus. And the greatest of these means is the Eucharist.

◆ One of the greatest sources of joy is learning to share in the joy of others.

◆ There are many daily occasions for experiencing joy, but we often pass them by unaware of their joy-producing possibilities because we have foolishly narrowed our expectations regarding what is a source of joy and what is not.

◆ St. Paul says to us: "I want you to be happy, always happy in the Lord; I repeat, what I want is your happiness...There is no need to worry; but if there is anything you need, pray for it, asking God for it with prayer and thanksgiving, and that peace of God, which is so much greater than we can understand, will guard your hearts and your thoughts, in Christ Jesus." (Phil 4: 4-7).

# On Union with Jesus

One of the above reflections on joy states that growth in joy depends on growth in our union with Jesus. One of our readers, Msgr. Bob Guste, in his book, *The Gift of the Church,* speaks to us convincingly concerning deep, personal relationship with Jesus: "Ideal Catholics held up to us by the Church are the *saints.* As you read their lives, what do you notice? One after the other, they were men and women who had a deep, personal relationship with Our Lord Jesus Christ. Their hearts were on fire with love for Him. Take a man like Ignatius of Loyola…Alphonsus Ligouri, with his brilliant mind, composed that prayer I learned as a child in Catholic school: 'I love You Jesus, my love. I love You more than myself. I repent with my whole heart for ever having offended You. Grant that I may love You always and then do with me what is Your will.'" A woman like Margaret Mary, to whom Our Lord appeared with His Heart ablaze with love, spent her life proclaiming the mystery of Jesus' personal love for each of us. Therese, called "the little flower of Jesus," died at the young age of 24. Under obedience, she wrote her autobiography, *The Story of a Soul.* Every page burns with love for Our Lord. One after the other, these men and women had a deep personal love for Jesus and, as a result, an ever growing love for all their sisters and brothers.

"Sometimes, for us Catholics, when we read these lives or hear them we think, "Well, that was okay for them but it's not for me! The Church honors them in order to say, 'Hey! It is for *you!*' We're all called to genuine holiness, as the Second Vatican Council reminds us. We're all called to grow every day in knowing, loving and serving Our Lord Jesus Christ. That's our goal, and everything we do in the Church is meant to foster that goal."[5]

# On Prayer Before the Tabernacle

Bishop Fulton Sheen, one of the most admired and influential speakers of this century, gives witness to the efficacy of praying before the Blessed Sacrament: "When I stand up to talk, people listen to me. They will follow what I have to say. St. Paul says: 'What do you have that was not given to you? And if it was given, how can you boast as though it were not?' (1 Cor 4:7). The secret of my power is that I have never in fifty-five years missed spending an hour in the presence of our Lord in the Blessed Sacrament. That's where the power comes from. That's where sermons are born. That's where every good thought is conceived."[6]

# The Priestly Character

The theologian Fr. Jean Galot, S.J., offers us some very meaningful words regarding the priestly character:

"Instead of seeking to demystify the priestly character, we should seek to discover the mystical significance it embodies, at least to the extent to which the term 'mystical' refers to the presence of mystery understood as God's plan of salvation taking hold of a man's life.

"Already at baptism and confirmation, this divine plan gains access to the depth of the human self and impresses upon it the project of the whole Christian life that is to unfold...The project God sketches out for the existence of a person does not remain confined solely to the person's will. It imprints itself onto the personal self, first through the baptismal character, then through that of confirmation, so that it may be realized from within.

"For the sake of precision, note that the priestly character is not added to the other two. It deepens the mark already there by imprinting upon the self

the project of a priestly life that is to come to fruition with the help of graces conferred during the exercise of the ministry. It impresses upon the being of the baptized person an orientation which commits the whole self to the mission of the priest.

Thus, this mission is not carried out from without, as when someone is sent by another to express a wish or convey an order. God engraves that mission in the very person. He makes it inseparable from personal being.

"Thus, we can well understand how the value of the priestly character is both ontological and dynamic. It is ontological because the priestly character affects personal being not more superficially than baptism—namely, only for the sake of a function to be exercised—but more thoroughly by bringing itself to bear upon the person's deepest feelings. It seeks to surrender to God, not only deeds, but the very source from which springs the doing of deeds, the human being itself with all its capacities and possibilities.

"Thus, in the character of order as in that of baptism and confirmation a new creation is entailed. Through the mark it imprints, ordination fashions a new being...

"The new being constituted by the character is not meant solely to raise the person to a level ontologically higher. Since it is intended for the sake of a mission that needs to be carried out, it is dynamic by its very nature. True, from this dynamic point of view, terms such as sign, seal, and mark fall short of the meaning intended. Of themselves, they do not do justice to what the character is destined to be, to its essential orientation toward action. In a doctrinal presentation, they must be supplemented by emphasizing the dynamism immanent in the mark imprinted on the soul.

"When we insist that the priesthood pertains to the order of being, this statement should not be taken to mean, not even by implication, that the priesthood pertains any less to the order of doing. The contrary is true. The priesthood engages us more radically at the level of our doing precisely because it affects what we are. In all this we recognize a distinctive sign that God is at work: He wants to gain possession of the whole person, and not only of the upper and visible layer, which is the person's activity. If the priest is to be capable of doing God's work, he must belong to God with his whole self. It is not in vain that he is called not merely God's messenger, but the man of God. Grasped by God in his whole being, he can radiate and communicate God by everything he is."[7]

# On the Joy of Being a Priest

Fr. Philip Hamilton, a former college professor and Air Force Chaplain, and now a pastor, speaks to us about the joy of being a priest:

"When I was a young priest as an assistant pastor in a rather large parish with a parish high school, I wore many hats.

"Everyone knows what an assistant pastor did...He had Sunday afternoon rosary and benediction of the Blessed Sacrament while the pastor listened to the Green Bay Packer football games. He was always late to his basketball practice on Tuesday nights because he had to give the Sorrowful Mother Novena. He taught a full load as teacher of Latin and religion in the parish high school...

"Sleep was not a major part of my life. Many a night I returned home at two in the morning from an athletic trip to be up for the six o'clock Mass the next morning.

What kept me going? The priesthood. Simply to be a priest was enough for us in those days. It was a cloud nine experience every day. I loved those boys and girls in Assumption High School...I hated getting up in the morning but it was worth it to offer Mass for those holy, appreciative, hardworking hospital sisters...

"If only our young men could understand the joys of being a priest, they would have to nail the front doors of the seminaries shut from the inside."[8]

# Act of Consecration

Lord Jesus, Chief Shepherd of the Flock, I consecrate my priestly life to Your Heart, pierced on Calvary for love of us. From Your pierced Heart the Church was born, the Church You have called me, as a priest, to serve in a most special way. You reveal Your Heart as symbol of Your love in all its aspects, including Your most special love for me whom You have chosen as Your priest-companion. Help me always to pour out my life in love of God and neighbor. Heart of Jesus, I place my trust in You!

Dear Blessed Virgin Mary, I consecrate myself to your maternal and Immaculate Heart, this Heart which is symbol of your life of love. You are the Mother of my Savior. You are also my Mother. You love me with the most special love as this unique priest-son. In a return of love I give myself entirely to your motherly love and protection. You followed Jesus perfectly. You are His first and perfect disciple. Teach me to imitate you in the putting on of Christ. Be my motherly intercessor so that, through your Immaculate Heart, I may be guided to an ever closer union with the pierced Heart of Jesus, Chief Shepherd of the Flock, who leads me to the Father in the Holy Spirit.

# The Holy Spirit in Our Lives

As the closing words of the act of consecration remind us, Jesus leads us to the Father in the Holy Spirit with Mary at our side. The Holy Spirit desires to fashion us into an ever greater likeness to Christ according to Jesus' pattern of death-resurrection. Mary our Mother cooperates with the Spirit, Whose spouse she is, in this process. Obviously, we should pray to the Holy Spirit each day. There are many ways we can do this. We can do this by simply turning over attention to the Spirit at various times during the day as we ask for His guidance. This method can also be complemented by saying certain established prayers. Here is one of these: "Come Holy Spirit, almighty Sanctifier. God of love, Who

filled the Virgin Mary with grace, Who wonderfully changed the hearts of the apostles, Who endowed all your martyrs with marvelous courage, come and sanctify us. Enlighten our minds, strengthen our wills, purify our consciences, rectify our judgment, set our hearts on fire, and preserve us from the misfortunes of resisting Your inspirations. Amen."

# Letters

We thank all those who have taken the time to write us. We very much appreciate your letters. Space limitations permit us to publish only a few of these:

A blessed New Year—and a quick note of thanks for the excellent bulletin, Shepherds of Christ.

Eamon Carroll, O. Carm.
Chicago, Illinois

I just wanted to drop you a note to tell you how much I enjoyed reading Shepherds of Christ. I found it good spiritual reading—and refreshing. Keep up the good work.

Sincerely in Christ,

Rev. Eugene P. Hruska, V.G.
Great Falls, Montana

NOTES:

1. Scriptural quotations are taken from *The Jerusalem Bible,* Doubleday & Company.
2. St. Thomas Aquinas, as in *The Liturgy of the Hours,* Catholic Book Publishing Co., Vol III, pp. 1335-1336.
3. Melito of Sardis, bishop, as in *The Liturgy of the Hours,* op. cit., Vol II, pp. 554-555.
4. St. Ambrose, as in *The Liturgy of the Hours,* op. cit., Vol II, p. 204.
5. Msgr. Bob Guste, *The Gift of the Church,* Queenship Publications, pp. 22-23.
6. *Through the Year with Fulton Sheen,* compiled by Henry Dietrick, Servant Books.
7. Jean Galot, S.J., *Theology of the Priesthood,* Ignatius Press, pp. 201-202.
8. Rev. Philip Hamilton, *Padre's Point,* Alt Publishing, pp. 44-46.

A Publication of
Shepherds of Christ
Ministries

# shepherds of Christ

## A SPIRITUALITY NEWSLETTER FOR PRIESTS

MAY/JUNE 1995

# Chief Shepherd of the Flock

"I am the Good Shepherd: the Good Shepherd is one who lays down His life for His sheep. The hired man, since he is not the shepherd and the sheep do not belong to him, abandons the sheep and runs away as soon as he sees a wolf coming, and then the wolf attacks and scatters the sheep. This is because he is only a hired man and has no concern for the sheep. I am the Good Shepherd. I know My own and My own know Me, just as the Father knows Me and I know the Father. And I lay down My life for My sheep." (Jn 10: 11-15[1]).

We have all seen many pictures of the Good Shepherd. Regarding those I myself have seen, I have come to the following conclusion: creating images

of the Good Shepherd seems to bring out the best in artists, at least in the majority of them. Most representations of the Good Shepherd I have seen are able to portray the love, the concern, the tenderness, and the strength of Jesus to an admirable degree.

Yes, Jesus the Good Shepherd reveals to us the above characteristics. He shows to all His love, concern, tenderness, and strength. But Jesus also reveals Himself to us on a most individual basis. He reveals Himself to me as my Savior—so loving, so concerned about me, so tender, so strong. He reveals Himself to me as the God-man Who longs to have a deep love relationship with me as this unique individual. What is my response? Is my response modeled after that of St. Paul, who realized Christ's gift of Himself in His passion and death was made for each of us in a most personal way, and, realizing this to the depths of his being, gave himself completely to Christ in the deepest love? Notice how personalized Paul makes the redemptive suffering and death and love of Jesus. In the letter to the

See *Chief Shepherd,* page 50, bottom

# Editor's Corner
by Edward Carter S.J.

This particular time of the year witnesses the ordination of young (and, more and more, not so young!) men to the priesthood. It is a time of happiness, when we rejoice with the newly ordained and with their parents and friends.

This time of the year, with its numerous ordinations, offers each of us who have been given the great gift of the priesthood an opportunity to reflect upon our own priestly existence. As we profusely thank God for the great gift of being a priest of Jesus Christ, we have the timely opportunity to ask ourselves how we have used our priestly existence, how we are using it now, and how we intend to use it in the future. We can ask ourselves these questions given to us by St. Ignatius Loyola: "What have I done for Christ? What am I doing for Christ? What ought I do for Christ?"

This time of the year also offers us an appropriate opportunity to resolve to begin to pray for priests on a daily basis—if we do not already do so. Here is a suggested prayer: "Lord Jesus, Chief Shepherd of the Flock, we pray that in the great love and mercy of Your Heart You attend to all the needs of Your priest-shepherds throughout the world. We ask that you draw back to Your Heart all those priests who have seriously strayed from Your path, that You rekindle the desire for holiness in the hearts of those priests who have become lukewarm, and that You continue to give Your fervent priests the desire for the highest holiness. United with Your priestly Heart and Mary's maternal Heart, we ask that You take this petition to your heavenly Father in the unity of the Holy Spirit."

---

*Chief Shepherd* continued from page 49

Galatians he does not use the plural but the singular: "I have been crucified with Christ, and I live now not with my own life but with the life of Christ who lives in me. The life I now live in this body I live in faith: faith in the Son of God who loved me and who sacrificed himself for my sake." (Gal 2:19-20).

# Reflections on Union with Jesus

The above considerations easily lead us to the following reflections:

◆ Jesus invites us but He does not coerce. He offers a religion which expands the person, not one which morbidly constricts. He offers us the fullness of life, but He does not say there will be no suffering involved. He wants us to live the human condition as His intimate friends.

◆ Living our life with Jesus is not meant to be a part-time occupation: "Whatever you eat, whatever you drink, whatever you do at all, do it for the glory of God." (1 Cor 10:31).

◆ To follow Jesus is not to lessen our being authentically human. Rather to follow Jesus allows us to be more human. In Christ we have a deepened, graced capacity to be human.

◆ Jesus has died and risen. We have been baptized into His death and resurrection. Each Christian act is characterized by this Christlike pattern. Whether we work or play, experience success or failure, are admired or ridiculed, taste ecstatic happiness or feel especially afflicted by the sorrowful aspect of human existence, we are dying and rising with Jesus.

◆ Why should the world's harsh dimension blind the Christian concerning its basic truth, goodness, and beauty? For to travel life's journey with this friend Jesus is to share His vision, a vision which permits us to see the world's Christlike image, which nothing—absolutely nothing—can destroy.

◆ Jesus loves each of us as precious, unique individuals. Allowing the realization of this simple but awesome truth to guide us is to walk the path which leads to the highest holiness.

◆ The committed Christian must consistently ask, "Is Jesus really the focal point of my existence?"

◆ "How many Christians really listen to Jesus' message and live it?" is a question I can ask but cannot answer. "How do I listen to Jesus' message and live it?" is a question I should ask and can answer.

◆ Jesus gathers up what are otherwise the all-too-fragmented pieces of my existence—the joy and the pain, the laughter and the tears, the success and the failure—and molds these into a Christlike unity.

◆ We are an enigma to ourselves when we seek happiness apart from the way of Jesus, knowing within the depths of our being that following such a path leads to hideous frustration.

◆ This or that person may not realize our present suffering. But Jesus knows—and He cares.

◆ The tender and reassuring touch of Jesus—we can vividly experience this in all sorts of situations, and sometimes when we least expect it.

◆ Jesus chose to lead much of His life in an obscure and disparaged place called Nazareth. This tells us something if we have ears with which to hear.

◆ It is sad but true that many Christians seem to have little or no desire for learning more about Jesus. Yet they eagerly pursue further knowledge concerning all sorts of other things. Let us pray for the grace never to be so blind.

◆ To grow in union with Jesus is to be increasingly possessed by His love. So possessed, we eagerly want to spend ourselves in love for God and neighbor, no matter what the cost.

◆ Jesus loved us and poured Himself out for us until there was no more to give. This is the poignant beauty of His life.

◆ How can we refuse to love anybody, since all have been touched by Jesus' redemptive blood?

◆ Jesus looked at me, and His gaze was so attractive. Jesus has reached out and touched me, and brought me to His Heart. This has been by happiness.

◆ Jesus has left His indelible imprint upon the human condition by the way He loved—in laughter and in tears, in work and in relaxation, in suffering and in rejoicing.

◆ At times we can refuse the voice of Jesus—we do not respond, we do not give, we do not grow in selflessness, we simply do not live as we should. Is it because of fear, or laziness, or sensuality, or pride, or rationalization?

◆ The acclaimed and the unnoticed, the lettered and the uneducated, the old and the young, the laborer and the scholar, the comely and the homely—people from all classes and situations have, over the ages, been inspired by the One called Jesus.

◆ His enemies have tried to stamp out the memory of Jesus. Yet He and His message are still vitally present, so much so that for countless persons life is meaningless without Him.

◆ Our own enthusiasm for Jesus can be aided by recalling the fervor of those who have preceded us in the cause of Christ. One of these, St. Ignatius of Antioch, wrote during the first ages of Christianity: "Neither the kingdoms of this world nor the bounds of the universe have any use for me. I would rather die for Jesus Christ than rule the last reaches of the earth. My search is for Him Who died for us; my love is for Him who rose for our salvation."[2]

◆ Jesus knows our weakness far better than we ourselves. Still He expects great things of us. Indeed, He has left us a unique formula, one that seems strange to the unbelieving: our weakness plus His strength can accomplish the marvelous, whether the marvelous be hidden or well-known, whether it appear to others as extremely important or seemingly insignificant.

◆ "My one hope and trust is that I shall never have to admit defeat, but that now as always I shall have the courage for Christ to be glorified in my body, whether by my life or by my death. Life to me, of course, is Christ, but then death would bring me something more…" (Ph 1:20-21).

# Thomas Merton on the Need for Silence

Here are some inspiring and insightful words of Thomas Merton on the need for prayerful silence in our lives:

"Silence does not exist in our lives for its own sake. It is ordered to something else. Silence is the mother of speech. A lifetime of silence is ordered to an ultimate declaration, which can be put into words, a declaration of all we have lived for.

"Life and death, words and silence, are given us because of Christ…In Him we die to illusion and live to truth. We speak to confess Him, and we are silent in order to meditate on Him and enter deeper into His silence, which is at once the silence of death and of eternal life—the silence of Good Friday night and the peace of Easter morning.

"We receive Christ's silence into our hearts when first we speak from our heart the word of faith. We work out our salvation in silence and in hope. Silence is the strength of our interior life. Silence enters into the very core of our moral being, so that if we have no silence we have no morality. Silence enters mysteriously into the composition of all the virtues, and silence preserves them from corruption.

"If we fill our lives with silence, then we live in hope, and Christ lives in us and gives our virtues much substance. Then, when the time comes, we confess Him openly before men, and our confession has much meaning because it is rooted in deep silence. It awakens the silence of Christ in the hearts of those who hear us, so that they themselves fall silent and begin to wonder and to listen. For they have begun to discover their true selves."[3]

# The Role of Private Revelation in the Life of the Church

In these our times there have been numerous reports from around the world of events regarding alleged private revelations. Messages from alleged visionaries and locutionists abound. Many people are at least somewhat confused regarding how one should react to all this.

It seems appropriate, therefore, to offer some thoughts concerning the role of private revelation in the life of the Church.

First of all, we must realize the Church recognizes that private revelation has a role to play in the life of the Church. The Catechism says:

"Throughout the ages, there have been so-called 'private revelations,' some of which have been recognized by the authority of the Church. They do not belong, however, to the deposit of faith. It is not their role to improve or complete Christ's definitive Revelation, but to help live more fully by it in a certain period of history."[4]

We would now like to offer the thoughts of some contemporary theologians regarding this role of private revelation: Harvey Egan, S.J., says: "Private revelations often presuppose the gift of prophecy. *Prophetic* revelations commission the mystic to address the entire Church, or a significant portion. He must deliver a message, plead for a particular devotion, call for conversion and penance, warn against certain aberrations in Church life...suggest new styles of life or spiritual doctrine, or foretell the future. Those post-apostolic, prophetic revelations, therefore, apply the faith in a practical way to daily Christian living."[5]

Jordan Aumann, O.P., observes: "There have always been persons gifted with prophecy, as is testified by Scripture and the processes of canonization of the servants of God. Nevertheless, private revelations do not pertain to the deposit of faith, which consists of the truths contained in Scripture and Tradition under the vigilance of the Church."[6]

Karl Rahner, S.J., offers the following regarding private revelation: "A private revelation as a mission to the Church signifies...an imperative which, within the context of a particular historical situation of the Church, points out a particular course of action from among the many possible according to the universal and public revelation as the one most urgently needing to be realized. The new feature in such a private revelation consists therefore not in its particular material elements but in the imperative marking and shifting of accentuation within the possibilities of Christianity...Hence the private revelation as a mission to the Church can be conceived as a heavenly imperative interpretation of the particular situation of the Church at this time; it answers the question as to what is most urgently to be done *here and now* in accordance with the general principles of the faith."[7]

It would be wrong, consequently, to deny the existence and proportionate importance of private revelation in the life of the Church. Such an attitude would be in opposition to the teaching of the Church and that of reputable theologians. Private revelation is yet another sign of God's overwhelming love towards us. In His great love He has given us the truths of faith as contained in public revelation. In His ongoing love for us He gives us private revelation to aid us in the living of public revelation. We should not, therefore, be indifferent to the role God has assigned to private revelation in the life of the Church.

It might be well at this point to offer a description of what occurs when a person receives an apparition and/or locution (message). Joseph de Guibert, S.J., one of the most eminent mystical theologians of this century, says:

"A distinction is made between corporeal, imaginative, and intellectual visions. This distinction can also be applied to locutions. In corporeal  visions and locutions there is a real perception by the external senses; the person who is seen or heard may be really present, or (in corporeal visions) the body which appears may be formed in the air, or a change may be affected at the moment the light-rays impinge on the eye, or (in corporeal locutions) a real acoustical vibration may be produced in the ears. In imaginative visions and locutions there is no perception by the external senses, but, rather, a Divine action on the imagination or the internal senses...In intellectual visions and locutions the Divine action directly affects the intellect."[8]

What should one's attitude be regarding alleged instances of private revelation which have not yet been the subject of official Church investigation— and perhaps never will be? First, one should always recognize that the final authority regarding private revelations rests with the Holy See of Rome, to whose judgment we should willingly submit. Secondly, one may personally act upon these messages of private revelation if a person observes that they contain nothing contrary to faith and morals and that they help bring one closer to God. Our Lord has said: "...a sound tree produces good fruit but a rotten tree bad fruit. A sound tree cannot bear bad fruit, nor a rotten tree bear good fruit." (Mt 7:17-18).

A good example of what we have just said is the situation regarding the alleged apparitions and messages at Medjugorje. The Church's investigation of this site is ongoing. No definitive decision has been made. In the meantime, the Church is *not* forbidding the faithful to go to Medjugorje. She is not forbidding them to personally accept the messages, presuming, again, they contain nothing contrary to faith and morals. Millions of pilgrims have gone to Medjugorje, including thousands of priests and hundreds of bishops.

An outstanding example of the importance of the role of private revelation in the life of the Church is that of Fatima. The Church has formally approved the message of Fatima as being worthy of belief. In her July 13, 1917, message, Our Blessed Mother said: "The war (World War I, then raging) is going to end. But if people do not stop offending God, another and worse one will begin in the reign of Pius XI. When you shall see a night illuminated by an unknown light (January 2, 1938), know that this is the great sign that God gives you that He is going to punish the world for its many crimes by means of war, hunger, and persecution of the Church and the

Holy Father.

"To prevent this, I shall come to ask for the consecration of Russia to my Immaculate Heart and the Communion of Reparation on the five first Saturdays. If my requests are granted, Russia will be converted and there will be peace. If not, she will scatter her errors throughout the world, provoking wars and persecutions of the Church. The good will be martyred, the Holy Father will have much to suffer, and various nations will be destroyed...

"But in the end, my Immaculate Heart will triumph, the Holy Father will consecrate Russia to me, Russia will be converted, and a certain period of peace will be granted to the world."[9]

There is more to the requests of Our Lady of Fatima besides those elements contained in the above message. But these aspects of the Fatima message are obviously critical ones.

Because enough people did not respond to Mary's requests made at Fatima, we did have World War II and all the horrors connected with the rise of Russian dominated Communism. Again, Fatima is a prime example of the importance the role of private revelation can assume in the life of the Church. Popes Pius XII and Paul VI made visits to Fatima, as has Pope John Paul II.

Concerning new apparitions, revelations, etc., there was an important decree issued under Pope Paul VI. This decree of the Congregation for the Propagation of the Faith A.A.S.58.1186 (approved by Pope Paul VI on October 14, 1966) states that the Imprimatur is no longer required on publications that deal with new revelations, apparitions, prophesies or miracles. It is presumed that such publications contain nothing contrary to faith and morals.

Here are some current messages of private revelation. Readers obviously are free to make up their own minds concerning them:

*Jesus:* "I want adoration of the Eucharist back. I want people to know I am God and I am coming to them in Holy Communion. I want the Blessed Sacrament exposed. I want My churches open. Union with Jesus, the love of Jesus, trust, faith, love for one another, love of God—I want all of these preached from the pulpit!

"You are under attack, My beloved priests, and you, in your busyness, are being led away from your union with Jesus. Bring yourselves back to Me and let Me give you My love...I wait for My beloved ones at the altar. I long for private union with My beloved ones.

"Come to Me, all who labor and are heavily burdened, and I will give you rest. Come and be lifted up to heights you never dreamed possible. I am God. Put your lives in My hands. Let me run your life. Bring your lives back to Jesus in the tabernacle."[10]

*Mary:* "Dear children! Today again, I want to call you to begin to live the new life from today onward. Dear children, I want you to comprehend that God has chosen each one of you in order to use you for the great plan of salvation of mankind. You cannot comprehend how great your role is in God's plan. Therefore, dear children, pray so that, through prayer, you may comprehend God's plan toward you. I am with you so that you can realize it completely."[11]

# St. Catherine of Sienna

Ignio Giordani offers us insightful thoughts concerning Catherine of Sienna, Saint and Doctor of the Church: "All the strivings of theologians and diplomats and preachers and missionaries are to no avail if they do not lead to love. By loving, one gives the life of God to the loved one. As St. John of the Cross will say: 'Where you do not find love, implant love and you will find love!' And Christ said to Catherine: 'He who knows himself to be loved cannot do otherwise than love; in loving he will put on the spirit of Christ crucified, and in the tempestuous sea of many troubles he will find himself at peace.'"[12]

Elsewhere, Giordani observes: "Man is like a candle to be lighted—to be lighted in God. The combustible material is love. As the heavenly Father will say to Catherine: 'Your material is love because I have created you for love; hence without love you cannot live.' Without love one must die: a lamp without oil goes out.

"This light is lighted day by day above all at the flame of the Eucharist, sacrament of love. 'The soul,' Jesus will say on another occasion to Catherine, 'receiving this Sacrament lives in me and I in it...'"[13]

# The Heart of Christ

June is the month especially dedicated to the Heart of Christ. In the preface of the Mass for the Solemn Feast of the Sacred Heart, the Church puts before us these words: "Lifted high on the cross, Christ gave his life for us, so much did he love us. From his wounded side flowed blood and water, the fountain of sacramental life in the Church. To his open heart the Savior invites all...to draw water in joy from the springs of salvation."[14] Who would want to refuse the Savior's invitation?

# Act of Consecration

Lord Jesus, Chief Shepherd of the Flock, I consecrate my priestly life to

Your Heart, pierced on Calvary for love of us. From Your pierced Heart the Church was born, the Church You have called me, as a priest, to serve in a most special way. You reveal Your Heart as symbol of Your love in all its aspects, including Your most special love for me, whom You have chosen as Your priest-companion. Help me always to pour out my life in love of God and neighbor. Heart of Jesus, I place my trust in You!

Dear Blessed Virgin Mary, I consecrate myself to your maternal and Immaculate Heart, this Heart which is symbol of your life of love. You are the Mother of my Savior. You are also my Mother. You love me with the most special love as this unique priest-son. In a return of love I give myself entirely to your motherly love and protection. You followed Jesus perfectly. You are His first and perfect disciple. Teach me to imitate you in the putting on of Christ. Be my motherly intercessor so that, through your Immaculate Heart, I may be guided to an ever closer union with the pierced Heart of Jesus, Chief Shepherd of the Flock, Who leads me to the Father in the Holy Spirit.

# The Holy Spirit in Our Lives

As the closing words of the act of consecration remind us, Jesus leads us to the Father in the Holy Spirit with Mary at our side. The Holy Spirit desires to fashion us into an ever greater likeness of Christ according to Jesus' pattern of death-resurrection. Mary our Mother cooperates with the Spirit, Whose spouse she is, in this process. Obviously, we should pray to the Holy Spirit each day. There are many ways we can do this. We can do this by simply turning our attention to the Spirit at various times during the day as we ask for His guidance. This method can also be complemented by saying certain established prayers. Here is one of these: "Come Holy Spirit, almighty Sanctifier. God of love, Who filled the Virgin Mary with grace, Who wonderfully changed the hearts of the apostles, Who endowed all your martyrs with miraculous courage, come and sanctify us. Enlighten our minds, strengthen our wills, purify our consciences, rectify our judgment, set our hearts on fire, and preserve us from the misfortunes of resisting Your inspirations. Amen."

# Letters

We thank all those who have taken the time to write us. We very much appreciate your letters. Space limitations permit us to publish only a few of these:

Dear Ed, I just wanted to take this chance to thank you for sending to me the Shepherds of Christ Newsletter. I have appreciated it very much, both to keep in touch with what you are doing and to enjoy the rich variety of topics needed for priestly reflection today—topics like friendship, prayer, and the Holy Spirit (a subject close to a Paulist's heart) in recent issues.

Sincerely,

Larry Boadt, CSP
Paulist Press, Mahwah, NJ

I like your newsletter very much. Shepherds of Christ gave me plenty of food for prayer!

Fr. Michael A. Becker
St. Rose of Lima, Altoona, PA.

NOTES:

1. Scriptural quotations are taken from *The New Jerusalem Bible,* Doubleday & Co.
2. "St. Ignatius of Antioch, The Letters," as in *The Fathers of The Church,* Fathers of the Church, Inc., p. 110.
3. *A Thomas Merton Reader,* Thomas McDonnell, editor, Doubleday, p. 459.
4. *The Catechism of the Catholic Church,* #67, p. 23.
5. Harvey Egan, S.J., *Christian Mysticism,* Pueblo Publishing, p. 311.
6. Jordan Aumann, O.P., *Spiritual Theology,* Our Sunday Visitor, Inc., p. 429.
7. Karl Rahner, S.J., *Theological Investigations,* Helicon Press, Vol. III, pp. 338-339.
8. Joseph de Guibert, S.J., *The Theology of the Spiritual Life,* Sheed & Ward, pp. 355-356.
9. *Our Lady of Fatima's Peace Plan from Heaven,* Tan Publishers, pp. 4-5.
10. *God's Blue Book: The Fire of His Love,* messages received by Rita Ring, Shepherds of Christ Publications, p.35.
11. Our Lady of Medjugorje, October 25, 1987, message as in *Live the Messages* by D.R. Golob, The Riehle Foundation.
12. Ignio Giordani, *Catherine of Sienna,* Bruce Publishing, p. 122.
13. Ibid., pp. 121-122.
14. *The Sacramentary,* Catholic Book Publishing Co., p. 463.

A Publication of
Shepherds of Christ
Ministries

# shepherds of Christ

## A SPIRITUALITY NEWSLETTER FOR PRIESTS

JULY/AUGUST 1995

Chief Shepherd of the Flock

# We Are Called to Imitate His Self-giving

"I am the Good Shepherd: the Good Shepherd is one who lays down His life for His sheep. The hired man, since he is not the shepherd and the sheep do not belong to him, abandons the sheep and runs away as soon as he sees a wolf coming, and then the wolf attacks and scatters the sheep. This is because he is only a hired man and has no concern for the sheep. I am the Good Shepherd. I know My own and My own know Me, just as the Father knows Me and I know the Father. And I lay down My life for My sheep." (Jn 10: 11 -15[1]).

He hung upon a cross on a hill called Calvary. Death was near. How much Jesus had already suffered! He had been brutally scourged. Much of His sacred body was a bloody, open wound. He had been derisively crowned with thorns. In a terribly weakened condition, He carried the heavy cross to the hill of Golgotha. There He was stripped of His garments and mercilessly nailed to the cross. After all this brutal and agonizing suffering, Jesus finally died.

Truly, the Good Shepherd had laid down His life for His sheep. That magnificent Heart, overflowing with love for His Father and all of us, had beat its last in a complete and magnificent act of self-giving: "When they came to Jesus, they found He was already dead, and so instead of breaking His legs one of the soldiers pierced His side with a lance. And immediately there came out blood and water. (Jn 19: 33-34).

Indeed, from the pierced Heart of Christ the Church with her sacraments was born. Two of these sacraments, the Eucharist and Baptism, are symbolized by the blood and water flowing from Christ's side. The sacrament of Orders was, of course, also born from the pierced Heart of Christ. We who are priests can never adequately thank Jesus for allowing us to receive this great and most special sacrament. The best way we can try to thank Him, though, is to utilize our priesthood to the fullest.

Each day we are called to imitate Jesus in His act of Self-giving. We, too, are called to lay down our lives for the flock. Relatively few priests in the

See *We Are Called,* page 62, bottom

# Editor's Corner
by Edward Carter S.J.

With this issue we begin our second year of publication of *Shepherds of Christ*. As with all new ventures, we've had our growing pains, and yet this first year has been a source of encouragement to us. We have had sufficient feedback from you our readers to allow us to realize that publishing the Newsletter is a very worthwhile endeavor. We feel that it is a great privilege to be able to provide an aid which can help priests grow in the spiritual life.

We live in very critical times for both the Church and the world. We priests, by our very vocation, are in a most advantageous position to make an extremely significant contribution to the betterment of both Church and world. And the more we grow spiritually, the more we are able to help the Church and the world.

We thank in a special way all those who have taken the time to write, encouraging us by telling us how the Newsletter is helping them and by offering suggestions which aid us in offering a better product. We also thank all those who have helped us financially through their thoughtful donations.

This particular issue, besides being the first one of our second year of publication, is also the first one published by Shepherds of Christ Ministries as an independent movement and tax-exempt organization. Until now we have been dependent upon Our Lady of Light Foundation. We wish to thank the Foundation for its indispensable assistance in our first year of existence. Shepherds of Christ Ministries, a movement dedicated to assisting in the renewal of the spiritual life, includes this newsletter for priests, other publications (including books and a spirituality newsletter for religious sisters and brothers), and a network of prayer chapters under the title, Shepherds of Christ Associates. The main purpose of the prayer chapters is to pray for all the needs of all priests the world over.

As we head into the second year of our existence, we fervently request your prayers for all aspects of Shepherds of Christ Ministries.

---

*We Are Called* continued from page 61
course of the Church's history have been called to lay down their lives in physical martyrdom. All priests, though, have been and are called to lay down their lives for the flock by giving themselves in loving service according to the Father's will.

Our act of self-giving occurs within the framework of common everydayness. We grow in Christian holiness within the framework of everyday life or we don't grow at all. This is such an obvious statement. It is one of those self-evident truths, a truth which no logical person would begin to challenge. Isn't it strange, then, that we can rather often fail to live this truth? Inexplicably, we so often seem to think that our real opportunity for growth in holiness—for self-giving in love—is not the opportunity which is everyday, but that opportunity which is in a kind of no man's land, an ethereal kind of opportunity removed from the ordinary pains and struggles and joys of everyday living, a nebulous opportunity which our hazy thinking really cannot pinpoint when we reflect upon the matter.

Our problem, then, is not that there is lacking ample opportunity for self-giving in love, for growth in holiness. Our problem rather is that we have a tendency to want different opportunities than everydayness presents.

Our task is to allow faith, hope, and love to be more vital, more operative, day-by-day, everyday. The more mature our Christian faith, hope, and love become, the more we will look upon each day as a renewed opportunity for self-giving in union with Jesus. We will increasingly come to see with a clearer vision that the opportunities for growth in priestly holiness, for growth in union with Jesus, Chief Shepherd of the Flock, are inserted deeply and firmly within the framework of everydayness. Yes, that's where they exist, and in bountiful measure.

# Thoughts on the Eucharist

The Self-giving of Jesus on Calvary is perpetuated in the Eucharist. The Eucharist is the chief source of our growth in self-giving. There follow various thoughts on the Eucharist which can deepen our appreciation of this magnificent gift of Jesus to us:

◆ "Then he took some bread, and when he had given thanks, broke it and gave it to them, saying, 'This is my body which will be given for you; do this as a memorial of me.' He did the same with the cup after supper, and said, 'This cup is the new covenant in my blood which will be poured out for you.'" (Lk 22: 19-20).

◆ The *Directory on the Ministry and Life of Priests* offers us this vivid reminder concerning the connection between the Eucharist and the priest's identity: "The sacramental memorial of the Death and Resurrection of Christ, the true and efficacious representative of the singular redemptive sacrifice, source and apex of Christian life in the whole of evangelization, the Eucharist is the beginning, means, and end of the priestly ministry, since all ecclesiastical ministries and works of the apostolate are bound up with the Eucharist and are directed towards it. Consecrated in order to perpetuate the Holy Sacrifice, the priest thus manifests, in the most evident manner, his identity."[2]

◆ One of our readers, Fr. Maynard Kolodziej, O.F.M., in his booklet, *Understanding the Mass,* reminds us of the connection between the Eucharist and the Old Testament Passover. "As the Israelites belonged to the People of God through circumcision, so we belong to the People of God through baptism. As the Israelites shared in the benefits of the old covenant by participating in the Passover celebration, so we share in the benefits of the new covenant by participating in the new Passover celebration, the Eucharist."[3]

◆ St. Peter Julian Eymard, founder of the Blessed Sacrament Fathers, gives us these bold words concerning Eucharistic devotion: "How is it that our Lord is so little loved in the Eucharist?

"One reason is that we do not speak enough of it and that we insist only on faith in the presence of Jesus Christ in the Most Blessed Sacrament instead of speaking about His life and His love therein...in a word, instead of showing Jesus Eucharistic with the personal and special love He has for each one of us.

"Another reason is our behavior, which denotes little love in us. From the way we pray, adore, and visit Him, no one would suspect the presence of Jesus Christ in our churches.

"How many among the best Catholics never pay a visit of devotion to the Most Blessed Sacrament to speak with Him from the Heart, to tell Him their love! They do not love our Lord in the Eucharist because they do not know Him well enough.

"But if, in spite of knowing Him and His love and the sacrifices and desires of His Heart, they still do not love Him, what an insult! Yes, an insult!

"For it amounts to telling Jesus Christ that He is not beautiful enough, not good enough, not lovable enough to be preferred to what they love.

"What ingratitude!

"After having received so many graces from this good Savior, made so many promises to love Him, and offered themselves so often to His service, such a treatment of Him is a mockery of His love.

"What cowardice!

"For if they do not want to know Him too well, to see Him at close quarters, to receive Him, to have a heart-to-heart talk with Him, the reason is they are afraid of being caught by His love. They fear being unable to resist His kindness; they fear being obliged to give in, to sacrifice their heart unreservedly, and their mind and life unconditionally.

"They are afraid of the love of Jesus Christ in the Most Blessed Sacrament, and they avoid Him.

"They are disturbed in His presence; they are afraid of yielding. Like Pilate and Herod they avoid His presence."[4]

◆ The Eucharist is not only a very special contact with God in Christ. In Christ we also relate to the other members of the Church. In receiving the Eucharist we pledge ourselves to deepen our love-union with all members of the Body which is the Church. We pledge to use these means which foster union. We determine to avoid that which causes selfish divisiveness.

The Eucharist also reminds us of our relationship with the entire human family. Jesus died and rose for all. The Eucharistic making-present of this paschal mystery nourishes our determination to assist in the work of ongoing redemption. The light of the Eucharist points to what we should be doing. The strength of the Eucharist assists us to so act in behalf of all.

The Eucharist, then, possesses the richest capacity to help us maintain and develop our personal relationship with God, the members of the Church, and all other members of the human family. And it will do just this *if* we surrender to its love, its power, its beauty.

◆ Henri Nouwen observes: "Jesus is God-for-us. Jesus is God giving himself completely, pouring himself out for us without reserve. Jesus doesn't hold back or cling to his own possessions…He gives all this to us…'Eat, drink, this is My body, this is My blood…this is Me for you!'"5

# Clarification on the Priestly Character

I wish to thank Fr. Valentine Young, O.F.M., for calling our attention to an ambiguous statement contained in the Jean Galot excerpt on the priestly character, which quotation appeared in the March-April, 1995 issue.

Taken by itself the passage in question can be confusing, leading one to ask whether Galot holds that the priestly character is distinct from those of Baptism and Confirmation. However, if the particular passage is taken within the context of the entire excerpt, I hope it is sufficiently clear—although perhaps not as clear as one would like—that Galot does hold the priestly character to be distinct from those of Baptism and Confirmation. This is certainly the explicit teaching of the Church—a teaching to which I firmly adhere. If I were doing that particular issue of the Newsletter here and now, I would omit the ambiguous passage. I apologize for any confusion I may have caused.

—*The Editor*

# Reflections on Community

The Eucharist is our chief source of growth in community. Each time we grow through the Eucharist we grow in the capacity to relate more deeply in love with the members of the Christian community as well as all others.

Here are some reflections and comments on community:

◆ "Now you together are Christ's body; but each of you is a different part of it." (1 Cor 12: 27).

◆ I need you, you need me. Why at times do we pretend that it is otherwise?

◆ John Downe, the British writer, far back in the seventeenth century, wrote these perennially applicable words: "No man is an island, entire of itself: every man is a piece of the continent, a part of the maine."[6]

◆ To expect the community which is the Church to be without sins and blemishes is to demand too much. On the other hand, to want the Church humbly to labor at a vigorous, ongoing conversion is to desire what the Spirit Himself wishes.

◆ Any form of Christian community must gaze inwardly upon itself in order to maintain and promote Spirit-inspired vitality. But if there is not a self-transcendence involved—a loving and concerned gaze outwardly toward the entire human family—then there is something tragically lacking.

◆ Fr. Ladislaus Orsy, S.J., says: "There are, there were, and there will be weaknesses in the Church. What should be the response of a Christian? It cannot be anything else than the Christian response that is compassion. Bitter criticism and aggressive accusation do not heal wounds. If anything, they aggravate the condition of the sick. Besides, those attitudes hardly proceed from faith, hope and love."[7]

◆ The little black boy and the little white boy hug each other in playful glee. How often little children can teach us—if we're not too stubborn and supercilious to listen.

◆ Needlessly to hurt another is simultaneously to hurt myself.

◆ St. Clement, Pope, writes to the Corinthians: "Why are there strife and passion, schisms and even war among you? Do we not possess the same spirit of grace which was given to us and the same calling in Christ? Why do we tear apart and divide the body of Christ? Why do we revolt against our own body? Why do we reach such a degree of insanity that we forget that we are members one of another?...

"We should put an end to this division immediately. Let us fall down before our master and implore his mercy with our tears. Then he will be reconciled to us and restore us to the practice of brotherly love that befits us...A person may be faithful; he may have the power to utter hidden mysteries; he may be discriminating in the evaluation of what is said and pure in his actions. But the greater he seems to be, the more humbly he ought to act, and the more zealous he should be for the common good rather than his own interest."[8]

◆ God has created each person as marvelously unique. He has also made us social beings. Each one's uniqueness, therefore, is meant to unfold within the framework of community.

◆ Fr. Avery Dulles, S.J., says, "The Church is a sign. It must signify in a historically tangible form the redeeming grace of Christ. It signifies that grace as relevantly given to…every age, race, kind, and condition. Hence the Church must incarnate itself in every human culture."[9]

◆ Community is often built through pain-demanding and time-demanding effort. How quickly, though, one can harm community through the uncharitable, cutting, and divisive word.

◆ To walk the path of life hand in hand with my brothers and sisters is Spirit-inspired wisdom. To want to walk alone is childish and pain-inflicting folly.

◆ Some are guilty because they unjustly use the structures and institutions of society variously to harm their fellowmen. Others are guilty because they neglect their responsibility to aid in reforming and strengthening these same social structures.

◆ Do I sincerely rejoice in the good others do? If not, why not? Community thrives on such rejoicing.

◆ The Christian community is intended to be a terrestrial reflection of that ultimate and perfect community—the Trinitarian life of Father, Son, and Holy Spirit.

◆ "If our life in Christ means anything to you, if love can persuade at all, or the Spirit that we have in common, or any tenderness and sympathy, then be united in your convictions and united in your love, with a common purpose and a common mind. That is the one thing which would make me completely happy. There must be no competition among you, no conceit; but everybody is to be self-effacing. Always consider the other person to be better than yourself, so that nobody thinks of his own interests first but everybody thinks of other people's interests instead." (Phil 2: 1-4).

# Pope John Paul II and Human Rights

From his recently published and best selling book, *Crossing the Threshold of Hope,* John Paul II gives us these insightful words which continue our theme on self-giving in union with Jesus:

"Therefore, these two aspects—the affirmation of the person as a person and the sincere gift of self do not exclude each other—they mutually confirm and complete each other. *Man affirms himself most completely by giving of himself.* This is the fulfillment of the commandment of love. This is also the full truth about man, a truth that Christ taught us by His life, and that the tradition of Christian morality, no less than the tradition of saints and of the many heroes of love of neighbor, took up and lived out in the course of history.

"If we deprive *human freedom* of this possibility, if man does not commit himself to becoming a gift for others, then this freedom can become dangerous. It will become freedom to do what I myself consider as good, what brings me a profit or pleasure, even a sublimated pleasure. *If we cannot accept the prospect of giving ourselves as a gift, then the danger of a selfish freedom will always be present.* Kant fought against this danger, and along the same line so did Max Scheler and so many after him who shared his ethics of values. But a complete expression of all this is already found in the Gospel. For this very reason, *we can find* in the Gospel a consistent declaration of all human rights, even those that for various reasons can make us feel uneasy."[10]

# Wisdom of the Saints

The Saints are ones who have achieved a self-giving in love to an outstanding degree. Their teaching is given to us as an aid in our own quest for the highest self-giving in union with Christ.

**St. Ignatius of Antioch:** "At last I am well on the way to being a disciple. May nothing, seen or unseen, fascinate me, so that I may happily make my way to Jesus Christ! Fire, cross, struggles with wild beasts, wrenching of bones, mangling of limbs, crunching of the whole body, cruel tortures inflicted by the devil—let them come upon me, provided only I make my way to Jesus Christ."[11]

**St. John of the Cross:** "What does it profit you to give God one thing if He asks for another? Consider what it is God wants and then do it."[12]

**St. Teresa of Avila.** In the following words from her classic work, *The Interior Castle,* Teresa is speaking of those who seek to bypass the humanity of Jesus in their prayer: "How much more is it necessary not to withdraw through one's own efforts from all our good and help which is the most sacred humanity of our Lord Jesus Christ. I cannot believe that these souls do so, but they just don't understand; and they will do harm to themselves and to others."[13]

**St. Bernard:** "I said in the beginning: the reason for our loving God *is* God. I spoke the truth, for He is both prime mover of our love and final end. He is Himself our human love's occasion; He also gives the power to love, and brings desire to its consummation. He is Himself the Lovable...and gives Himself to be the object of our love...How kindly does He lead us in love's way, how generously He returns the love we

**Heart of Jesus, We place our trust in You.**

give, how sweet He is to those who wait for Him!"[14]

**St. Francis of Assisi:** "Our Lord says in the Gospel, *Love your enemies.* A man really loves his enemy when he is not offended by the injury done to himself, but for love of God feels burning sorrow for the sin his enemy has brought on his own soul."[15]

"We can never tell how patient or humble a person is when everything is going well with him. But when those who should cooperate with him do the exact opposite, then we can tell. A man has as much patience and humility as he has then, and no more."[16]

"Blessed are the peacemakers, for they shall be called the children of God. They are truly peacemakers who are able to preserve their peace of mind and heart for love of our Lord Jesus Christ, despite all that they suffer in this world."[17]

**St. Ignatius of Loyola.** "It is characteristic of God and His Angels, when they act upon the soul, to give true happiness and spiritual joy, and to banish all the sadness and disturbances which are caused by the enemy.

"It is characteristic of the evil one to fight against such happiness and consolation by proposing fallacious reasonings, subtleties, and continual deceptions.

"In souls that are progressing to greater perfection, the action of the good angel is delicate, gentle, delightful. It may be compared to a drop of water penetrating a sponge.

"The action of the evil spirit upon such souls is violent, noisy and disturbing. It may be compared to a drop of water falling upon a stone.

"In souls that are going from bad to worse, the action of the spirits mentioned above is just the reverse. The reason for this is to be sought in the opposition or similarity of these souls to the different kinds of spirits. When the disposition is contrary to that of the spirits, they enter with noise and commotion that are easily perceived. When the disposition is similar to that of the spirits, they enter silently, as one coming into his own house when the doors are open."[18]

**St. Benedict.** The following words are from the Rule of St. Benedict. Although they directly pertain to life in the monastery, they are profitable for all, for they breathe the spirit of peace so central to Benedictine spirituality: "...and so we are going to establish a school for the service of the Lord. In founding it we hope to introduce nothing harsh or burdensome. But if a certain strictness results from the dictates of equity for the amendment of vices or the preservation of charity, do not be at once dismayed and fly from the way of salvation, whose entrance cannot but be narrow, for as we advance in the religious life and in faith, our hearts expand and we run the way of God's commandments with unspeakable sweetness of love. Thus, never departing from His school, but persevering in the monastery according to His teaching until death, we may by patience share in the sufferings of Christ and deserve to have a share also in His kingdom."[19]

**St. Dominic.** From *Various Writings on the History of the Order of Preachers* we have these words concerning St. Dominic: "Dominic possessed such great integrity and was so strongly motivated by divine love, that without a doubt he proved to be a bearer of honor and grace. He was a man of great equanimity, except when moved to compassion and mercy. And since a joyful heart animates the face, he displayed the peaceful composure of a spiritual man in the kindness he manifested outwardly and by the cheerfulness of his countenance."[20]

**St. Jean Vianney.** "What keeps us priests back from the attainment of holiness is lack of consideration. It displeases us to withdraw our minds from outside things. We do not know what we rightly do. We have need of intimate reflection, continuous prayer and intimate union with God."[21]

# A Priest Holds His Ground

The gift of self in Christ demands holding true to one's principles even though this is at times an unpopular stance. Fr. Phil Hamilton, a former college professor and Air Force Chaplain, and now a Pastor, has spoken to us in previous newsletters. Here are further words of his from his book, *Padre's Point.* They remind us of the necessity of holding one's ground: "I as a priest have at times been accused of 'coming on too strong,' and thus 'turning people off.' Some students have accused me of this, and have, therefore, not registered for any of my classes. In parish life I have experienced people getting up and walking out of my office in the middle of a discussion. This is a very infrequent happening, but still it causes me to think.

"My general philosophy that I have expressed to my students and in counseling through the years is 'people can be tilted, but not shoved.' In all my years in the priesthood I have never claimed that I have really changed anyone. I only tilt someone occasionally toward what I think is the true course to be pursued in life. It is, therefore, a traumatic experience for me to be accused of being a 'shover.' The more literate would say I am too doctrinaire.

"My mother, Aggie Murphy Hamilton, brought us kids up on the principle that 'God and one constitute a majority.' I unreservedly believe in the teaching of Christ as presented to me through an infallible Church. I suppose such a background would influence one in presenting a rather, 'he always thinks he is right,' doctrinaire image to the modern world where everything is up for grabs, where no one is sure of anything morally or doctrinally.

"And so I have a problem relating. But so likewise does the Church, and so likewise the family. Business does not have such a problem. You can't individually fight the boss except through the courts. The state does not have the problem, because its courts can always say 'this is the law,' and if you violate their decision, they can throw you in the slammer.

"But the rest of us have the problem. How to react? When we know we are right from Church teaching, experience, or common sense, we must be true to our principles. We must have the courage and strength to say both what is true and false. To do anything else is to prostitute one's integrity for the sake of acceptance."[22]

# On Being Relevant

These thoughts on relevancy easily follow the ideas of Fr. Hamilton.

◆ That which is relevant is appropriate or germane, fitting for the matter at hand. We see, then, that Jesus lived the perfectly relevant life, since he always did the perfectly appropriate thing according to His Father's will. We see a paradox, then. Many reject Jesus as being irrelevant, and yet He is the supremely relevant One. The relevancy of His life and message is perennial.

◆ Despite what others may think, when we act in accord with the Christlike self, we are being relevant.

◆ Christian relevancy does indeed mean that we must read the signs of the times as we preach and live the Gospel message. In doing so, however, we must be careful not to engage in the Gospel's betrayal.

◆ Sometimes that which is most traditional is the most relevant; at other times, that which is most new. We must have the courage to choose accordingly.

◆ St. Paul had something to say about Christian relevancy: "For Christ did not send me to baptize, but to preach the Good News, and not to preach that in the terms of philosophy in which the crucifixion of Christ cannot be expressed. The language of the cross may be illogical to those who are not on the way to salvation, but those of us who are on the way see it as God's power to save...And so, while the Jews demand miracles and the Greeks look for wisdom, here are we preaching a crucified Christ; to the Jews an obstacle that they cannot get over, to the pagans madness, but to those who have been called, whether they are Jews or Greeks, a Christ who is the power and the wisdom of God..." (1 Cor 1: 17-24).

# On Prayer

Prayer is a most necessary means for growth in the gift of self. Here are some thoughts on prayer:

◆ Fr. Henri Nouwen, one of the best known spiritual writers of our times, offers us the following:

"For a man of prayer is, in the final analysis, the man who is able to recognize in others the face of the Messiah and make visible what was hidden, make touchable what was unreachable. The man of prayer is a leader precisely because through his articulation of God's work within himself he can lead others out of confusion to clarification; through his compassion he can guide them out of the closed circuits of their ingroups to the wide world of humanity, and through his critical contemplation he can convert their convulsive destructiveness into creative work for the new world to come."[23]

And elsewhere Nouwen gives us this interesting story: "Not long ago I met a parish priest. After describing his hectic schedule—religious services, classroom teaching, luncheon and dinner engagement, and organizational meetings—he said apologetically, 'Yes, but there are so many problems.' When I asked, 'Whose problem?,' he was silent for a few minutes, and then more or less reluctantly said, 'I guess my own.' Indeed, his incredible activities seemed in large part motivated by fear of what he would discover when he came to a standstill. He actually said, 'I guess I am busy in order to avoid a painful self-concentration.'"[24]

◆ We should not be afraid to look at ourselves, as the above described priest apparently was. Prayerful reflection upon myself in union with Jesus

will give me a growing sense of peace and security, resulting from an increased prayerful awareness of how much Jesus loves me as this unique priest-companion. If there is pain involved in prayerful self-reflection, the pain soon fades to the background. In prayer Jesus shows us how lovable we are. He loved us unto His brutal death. Redeemed by the love of God, how can we be unlovable? We have been salvifically touched by His redemptive blood. We are thus beautiful in His sight. His love for us continues, and the more we surrender to the boundless love of His magnificent Heart, the more the truth, the goodness, and the beauty of our person shine forth.

◆ St. Cyprien gives us these reflections on the Lord's Prayer:

"My dear friends, the Lord's Prayer contains many great mysteries of our faith. In these few words there is great spiritual strength, for this summary of divine teaching contains all of our prayers and petitions. And so, the Lord commands us: *Pray then like this: 'Our Father. who art in heaven.'*

"We are new men; we have been reborn and restored to God by his grace. We have already begun to be his sons and we can say 'Father.' John reminds us of this: *He came to his own home, and his own people did not receive him. But to all who received him, who believe in his name, he gave the power to become children of God.* Profess your belief that you are sons of God by giving thanks. Call upon God who is your Father in heaven."[25]

◆ Rosary Reflections:

*Joyful Mysteries: The Annunciation:* "The Father has a plan. Jesus was incarnate in the womb of the Virgin Mary. Jesus came to this earth in quietness. This was part of the Father's plan. Mary always complied with the Father's will. When she said, *'Be it done to me according to thy word,'* she was showing her willingness to do whatever the Father was asking her to do."

*Sorrowful Mysteries; The Scourging at the Pillar:* "They took Jesus, tied Him to a pillar and whipped Him with harsh instruments that tore His skin and made Him bleed. This is your friend, Jesus. He is God! He came to earth so that we might be with Him forever in heaven. See Him covered with wounds, deep wounds, His marks of love covering His entire body!"

*Glorious Mysteries: The Resurrection:* "Jesus walked with two disciples on the way to Emmaus and recounted for them all the scriptures in the Old Testament from the time of Moses that referred to Him. They did not understand that Jesus would die and then rise again. They did not recognize Him after He rose. You might think, 'oh, so blind were they! How could they not recognize Jesus?' But Jesus is in our midst this day. He is present right here with us. He is present in the tabernacle. He is present in us and in our world and the world continues to go on its way in blindness."[26]

# Laurentin and Mary

Fr. René Laurentin, one of the world's foremost Mariologists, offers us these meaningful words concerning Mary: "She was present physically throughout the life of Christ—both by her mother's love and by her commitment to him. It was a communion of faith, of hope and of charity. Mary's presence to her son is a model for us, since, through this mother, God becomes our brother and has given her to us as mother in order to identify us with himself...We are humble children of this mother who has so profoundly adopted us in him...Mary has the mission of aiding the work of our divinization in Jesus Christ. She cooperates with him in this work of God."[27]

# Act of Consecration

Lord Jesus, Chief Shepherd of the Flock, I consecrate my priestly life to Your Heart, pierced on Calvary for love of us. From Your pierced Heart the Church was born, the Church You have called me, as a priest, to serve in a most special way. You reveal Your Heart as symbol of Your love in all its  aspects, including Your most special love for me, whom You have chosen as Your priest-companion. Help me always to pour out my life in love of God and neighbor. Heart of Jesus, I place my trust in You!

Dear Blessed Virgin Mary, I consecrate myself to your maternal and Immaculate Heart, this Heart which is symbol of your life of love. You are the Mother of my Savior. You are also my Mother. You love me with the most special love as this unique priest-son. In a return of love I give myself entirely to your motherly love and protection. You followed Jesus perfectly. You are His first and perfect disciple. Teach me to imitate you in the putting on of Christ. Be my motherly intercessor so that, through your Immaculate Heart, I may be guided to an ever closer union with the pierced Heart of Jesus, Chief Shepherd of the Flock, Who leads me to the Father in the Holy Spirit.

# The Holy Spirit and the Priest

The *Directory on the Ministry and Life of Priests* reminds us of how closely

the priest is united to the Holy Spirit, of how the Holy Spirit is given to priests to lead us along the path of total self-giving: "In Priestly Ordination, the priest has received the seal of the Holy Spirit which has marked him by the sacramental character in order to always be the minister of Christ and the Church. Assured of the promise that the Consoler will abide 'with him forever' (Jn 14: 16-17), the priest knows that he will never lose the presence and the effective power of the Holy Spirit in order to exercise his ministry and live with charity his pastoral office as a total gift of self for the salvation of his own brothers."[28]

# Letters

We thank all those who have taken the time to write to us. We very much appreciate your letters. Space limitations permit us to publish only a few of these.

Dear Fr. Ed,

From nowhere I received a copy of your newsletter. Reading it was a source of simple delight as is anything buoying up our priesthood these days. The folksy "Joys of Being a Priest" (by Fr. Philip Hamilton, March-April issue) brought a smile. I think of these fifty-one years with their ups and downs as something very special. As life moves quickly and relentlessly on I am sure of this: *It Is Great To Be a Priest.* To have spent this one life on anything less would appear to this simple soul as a great waste. Please keep the newsletter coming—and thank you for the lift!

Fraternally in Christ,
Rev. Charles Mallen, C.Ss.R.
Venice, Florida

Dear Ed,

It is slow in coming, but I want to add my voice to the praise your newsletter for priests must be getting. I find the material good for reflective, meditative reading and praying. Heaven knows we priests need that.

In the Heart of Christ,
Bob Harvanek, S.J.
Loyola University, Chicago

Dear Fr. Ed,

Of all the stuff that comes cascading into my mailbox every day, "Shepherds of Christ" really stands out. To me it exemplifies one of the great strengths of Catholicism—its spirituality. I use the newsletter for my prayer after Mass. It has brought me closer to God through Christ by focusing on the basics of Catholic-Christian spirituality in a way that enlightens and inspires.

Fr. Bill Zimmer
Chicago, Illinois

NOTES:
1. Scriptural quotations are taken from *The Jerusalem Bible,* Doubleday & Co.
2. *Directory on the Ministry and Life of Priests,* as in special supplement, *Inside the Vatican,* p. 181.
3. Maynard Kolodziej, O.F.M., *Understanding the Mass,* Franciscan Publishers, p. 31.
4. *The Treasury of Catholic Wisdom,* ed., John Hardon, S.J., Ignatius Press, p. 582.
5. Henri Nouwen, *With Burning Hearts,* Orbis Books, p. 67.
6. John Donne, "Devotions Upon Emergent Occasions," XVII, as in *John Donne, Complete Poetry and Selected Prose,* ed., John Hayward, The Nonesuch Press, p. 538.

7. Ladislaus Orsy, S.J., "On Being One with the Church Today," *Studies in the Spirituality of Jesuits*, Vol. VII, January.
8. St. Clement, Pope, from a letter to the Corinthians, as in *The Liturgy of the Hours*, Catholic Book Publishing Co., Vol. III, pp. 455-456.
9. Avery Dulles, *Models of the Church*, Doubleday, p. 63.
10. Pope John Paul II, *Crossing the Threshold of Hope*, Alfred A. Knopf, p. 202.
11. St. Ignatius of Antioch, "Ignatius to the Romans," as in *The Treasury of Catholic Wisdom*, op.cit., p. 14.
12. St. John of the Cross, "Sayings of Light and Love," No. 70, as in *The Treasury of Catholic Wisdom*, op. cit., p. 495.
13. St. Teresa of Avila, "The Interior Castle," Bk. VI, Ch. 7, as in *The Collectible Works of St. Teresa of Avila*, tr., Kieran Kavanaugh, O.C.D., and Otilio Rodriguez, O.C.D., ICS Publications, Vol. II, p. 399.
14. St. Bernard, "On the Love of God," as in *The Treasury of Catholic Wisdom*, op. cit., p. 193.
15. St. Francis of Assisi, "The Admonitions," No. IX, as in *The Treasury of Catholic Wisdom*, op. cit., p.217.
16. Ibid., No. XIII, p. 218.
17. Ibid., No. XV, p. 219.
18. *The Spiritual Exercises of St. Ignatius*, Newman Press, Nos. 329, 335.
19. "The Rules of St. Benedict," Prologue, as in *The Treasury of Catholic Wisdom*, p. 165.
20. "From the Various Writings of the History of the Order of Preachers," as in *The Liturgy of theHours*, Catholic Book Publishing Co., Vol. IV, p. 1302.
21. Pope John XXIII, *The Curé of Ars and the Priesthood*, Encyclical Letter, Paulist Press, p. 16.
22. Philip Hamilton, *Padre's Point*, Alt Publishing Co., pp. 117-118.
23. Henri Nouwen, *The Wounded Healer*, Doubleday, p. 47.
24. Ibid., p. 90.
25. St. Cyprien, as in *The Liturgy of the Hours*, Catholic Book Publishing Co., Vol. III, p. 359.
26. *God's Blue Book, Rosary Meditations*, Rita Ring, to be published by Shepherds of Christ Publications.
27. René Laurentin, *A Year of Grace with Mary*, Veritas Publications, pp. 113-114.
28. *Directory on the Ministry and Life of Priests*, op. cit., p. 61.

A Publication of
Shepherds of Christ
Ministries

# shepherds of Christ

## A SPIRITUALITY NEWSLETTER FOR PRIESTS

SEPTEMBER/OCTOBER 1995

### Chief Shepherd of the Flock

# Trust in the Lord

"I am the good shepherd: the good shepherd is one who lays down his life for his sheep. The hired man, since he is not the shepherd and the sheep do not belong to him, abandons the sheep and runs away as soon as he sees a wolf coming, and then the wolf attacks and scatters the sheep. This is because he is only a hired man and has no concern for the sheep. I am the good shepherd. I know my own and my own know me, just as the Father knows me and I know the Father. And I lay down my life for my sheep." (Jn 10: 11 -15[1]).

The fact that Jesus the Good Shepherd has laid down His life for each and every one of us should fill us with the greatest confidence, with the greatest trust. As St. Paul tells us: "We were still helpless when at His appointed moment Christ died for sinful men. It is not easy to die, even for a good man—though, of course, for someone really worthy, a man might be prepared to die—but what proves that God loves us is that Christ died for us while we were still

*Heart of Jesus, We place our trust in You.*

sinners. Having died to make us righteous, is it likely that He would now fail to save us from God's anger? When we were reconciled to God by the death of His Son, we were still enemies; now that we have been reconciled, surely we may count on being saved by the life of His Son? Not merely because we have been reconciled but because we are filled with joyful trust in God, through our Lord Jesus Christ, through whom we have already gained our reconciliation." (Rm 5: 6-11).

Those words of Paul remind us that we have every motive to have the greatest trust in Our Lord. One of the major reasons we fail to progress in the spiritual life as we should is that our trust is deficient. We should pray for an increase in this extremely important virtue each day of our lives. We should pray for an increased awareness of how much Jesus loves us as unique individuals. The more I am convinced how much Jesus loves me, the easier it is to surrender to Him in trust.

# Editor's Corner
by Edward Carter S.J.

I would like to begin this column by sharing with you material from two letters we have recently received.

Fr. Vaughn Winters writes from St. Raphael's Church, Santa Barbara, California: "Thank you for giving of yourself to minister to priests throughout the country through the Shepherds of Christ newsletter. As a priest just two years ordained, sometimes when I look around and see so many troubled priests, and also hear dire forebodings about the coming priest shortage, I wonder what I've gotten myself into, but your newsletter helps me refocus on what it is all about, and also a reminder that I am part of a vast fraternity of many healthy, solid, and holy priests. Thank you for your ministry of encouragement and strengthening." And thank you, Fr. Winters, for your inspiring words!

The following is part of a letter from Fr. Guillermo Arias, S.J., who has volunteered to help us distribute the newsletter in Puerto Rico: "I...thank and praise the Good Lord...for having inspired you and your associates to begin this most urgent apostolate among Christ's priests...You are doing one of the most important services anyone can do for the Church today with Shepherds of Christ Ministries. And I would like to be of as much help as possible." And thank you, Fr. Arias!

The above continues the feedback we have received which helps assure us that the Lord has given us a very important ministry. We would very much appreciate your prayers for the continued success of this ministry.

Also, with this issue we are making a special plea for your financial assistance. As you know, the newsletter is sent to you free of charge, although donations are always welcome. Our expenses are paid through donations received from the laity and yourselves. At this particular time, we are making it especially easy for you to financially assist Shepherds of Christ Ministries—and the chief expense of this movement is the publication of the priests' newsletter. Our expenses are increasing as we are now beginning to distribute the newsletter in other countries. Enclosed you will find a self-addressed reply envelope for donation purposes. Thank you very much for taking our appeal under consideration.

# Reflections on Trust

There follow further thoughts on the attitude of trust which we should strive to possess in greatest measure:

◆ Trust does not always come easily. Especially in times of great difficulty or crisis we can experience the difficulty of trusting properly in God. Yet it is precisely then that we have a special need for trust. Despite the suffering, we must trust, even though the darkness may enshroud us. We must try to trust as did Abraham: "Though it seemed Abraham's hope could not be fulfilled, he hoped and he believed, and through doing so he did become *the father of many nations* exactly as he had been promised: *Your descendants will be as many as the stars.* Even the thought that his body was past fatherhood—he was about a hundred years old—and Sarah too old to become a mother, did not shake his belief. Since God had promised it, Abraham refused either to deny it or even to doubt it, but drew strength from faith and gave glory to God, convinced that God had power to do what he had promised." (Rm 4:18-21).

◆ God can accomplish great things through us, too, if only we allow Him. What He accomplishes through us may be for the most part hidden from others, yet true greatness can still be there. But if we are to achieve truly great things, we must trust. We must trust that God will lead us on to Christian maturity. We must trust that He will aid us in the fulfillment of our roles in life. Even at those times when we are painfully aware of how weak we are, we must trust that we can attain true greatness and accomplish the task God sets before us. Actually, at those times during which we are especially experiencing our weakness, our optimism should grow. For the more we realize our weakness, the more we should throw ourselves into the arms of Christ. We then become strong and secure in His strength. As long as we do not surrender to our weakness, we should glory in our helplessness so that the strength of Christ may support us. This was the attitude of St. Paul: "So I shall be very happy to make my weaknesses my special boast so that the power of Christ may stay over me, and that is why I am quite content with my weaknesses, and with insults, hardships, persecutions, and the agonies I go through for Christ's sake. For it is when I am weak that I am strong." (2 Cor 12: 9-10).

◆ If our days are too much colored with discouragement and pessimism, our trust has become dormant. We must rekindle it and tell ourselves that we belong to Jesus and that nothing, absolutely nothing, should destroy the basic peace and joy He desires for us.

◆ How fortunate that our Christian trust can carry us beyond the toil, the pain, the anxiety of the present moment.

◆ In times of distress we instinctively turn to Jesus, immediately realizing the need for trust. However, we do not so easily realize our need for Him during times when all goes smoothly and a sense of joy seems to touch every fiber of our being. Yet we need to be cognizant of our dependence on Jesus during these happy episodes. For, if during time of distress we need to trust in the Lord for patient endurance, during times of joy we are in no less need of His help. We must trust that He will give us the light and strength to use these periods of joy not selfishly, but as He wills.

◆ Why don't we decide once and for all to take Jesus at His word? He tells us not to worry. He tells us there is no reason to be overly anxious about anything. He tells us to trust. He loves us, His Father loves us, the Holy Spirit loves us. They love us much more than we love ourselves. Their love can cut through the bonds of any fear, any worry, any anxiety.

◆ Fr. Edward Leen, C.S.Sp., speaks about trust and spiritual childhood: "To be childlike is far different from being childish. Jesus was the one; He was anything but the other...

"A child's glance is always outwards. To keep one's eyes habitually turned towards God, as a child looks to its parent, is the way to self-oblivion. To commit ourselves wholly to God's paternal love, to put fearless childlike trust in His goodness, and to base all one's hopes of being in the Divine favor, in life and in death, in His fatherly loving kindness and mercy, is to have attained to a lofty degree of spiritual childhood."[2]

◆ Fr. Gordon Aumann, O.P., describes some of the characteristics of the virtue of trust in those far advanced in the spiritual life:

"*Universal confidence in God.* Nothing is able to discourage a servant of God when he or she enters upon an enterprise pertaining to the divine glory...

"*Indestructible peace and serenity.* This is a natural consequence of their universal confidence in God. Nothing can disturb the tranquility of their spirit. Ridicule, persecution, calumny, injury, sickness, misfortune—everything falls upon their souls like water on a stone, without leaving the slightest trace or alteration in the serenity of their spirit..."[3]

◆ In the diary of Blessed Faustina, we read these words given to her by Our Lord: "I have opened My Heart as a living fountain of mercy. Let all souls draw life from it. Let them approach this sea of mercy with trust...On the cross, the fountain of My mercy was opened wide by the lance for all souls—no one have I excluded!...The graces of My mercy are drawn by means of one vessel only, and that is trust. The more a soul trusts, the more it will receive."[4]

◆ St. Claude de la Columbière: "My God, I am so convinced that you keep watch over those who hope in You, and that we can want for nothing when we look for all from You, that I am resolved in the future to live free from every care, and to turn all my anxieties over to You...

"Men may deprive me of possessions and of honor, sickness may strip me of strength and the means of serving you...but I shall never lose my hope. I shall keep it till the last moment of my life; and at that moment all the demons in Hell shall strive to tear it from me in vain...

"Others may look for happiness from their wealth or their talents; others may rest on the innocence of their life, or the severity of their penance, or the amount of their alms, or the fervor of their prayers. As for me, Lord, all my confidence is my confidence itself. This confidence has never deceived anyone. No one, no one has hoped in the Lord and has been confounded.

"I am sure, therefore, that I shall be eternally happy, since I firmly hope to be, and because it is from You, O God, that I hope for it. I know, alas!, I know only too well, that I am weak and unstable. I know what temptation can do against the strongest virtue. I have seen the stars of heaven fall, and the pillars of the firmament; but that cannot frighten me. So long as I continue to hope, I shall be sheltered from all misfortune; and I am sure of hoping always, since I hope also for this unwavering hopefulness.

"Finally, I am sure I cannot hope too much in You, and that I cannot receive less than I hoped for from You. So I hope that you will hold me safe on the steepest slopes, that You will sustain me against the most furious assaults, and that You will make my weakness triumph over my most fearful enemies. I hope that You will love me always, and that I too shall love You without ceasing. To carry my hope once for all as far as it can go, I hope from You to possess You, O my Creator, in time and in eternity. Amen."[5]

# Thoughts on the Eucharist

The Eucharist is our chief source for growth in trust. We should pray for a deepened awareness of this magnificent Gift.

◆St. Peter Julian Eymard: "It is true also that the world does all in its power to prevent us from loving Jesus in the Most Blessed Sacrament with a real and practical love, to prevent us from visiting Him, and to cripple the effects of this love.

"The world engrosses the attention of souls; it finds and enslaves them with external occupations in order to deter them from dwelling too long on the love of Jesus.

"It even fights directly against this practical love and represents it as optional, as practicable at most only in a convent.

"And the devil wages incessant warfare on our love for Jesus in the Most Blessed Sacrament.

"He knows that Jesus is there, living and substantially present; that by Himself He is drawing souls and taking direct possession of them. The devil tries to efface the thought of the Eucharist in us, and the good impression made by it; for in his mind, that should decide the issue of the struggle.

"And yet God is all love.

"This gentle Savior pleads with us from the Host: 'Love Me as I have loved you; abide in My love! I came to cast the fire of love on the earth, and My most ardent desire is that it should set your hearts on fire.'"[6]

# The Heart of Christ

Jesus, in revealing His Heart as symbol of His life of love—including His overwhelming love for each of us as unique persons—invites us to have the greatest trust in Him. Here are some quotations which can help us in developing trust in the Heart of Christ:

◆ St. Bonaventure, Doctor of the Church, in his work *The Mystical Vine*, says: "The heart I have found is the heart of my King and Lord, of my Brother and Friend, the most loving Jesus. I say without hesitation that His Heart is also mine. Since Christ is my head, how could that which belongs to my head not also belong to me? As the eyes of my bodily head are truly my own, so also is the heart of my spiritual Head. Oh, what a blessed lot is mine to have one heart with Jesus!...Having found this heart, both yours and mine, O most sweet Jesus, I will pray to you my God."[7]

◆ Ludolph of Saxony, whose book *The Life of Jesus Christ* played a key role in the conversion of St. Ignatius Loyola, gives us these inspiring words from this very book regarding the Heart of Christ: "The Heart of Christ was wounded for us with the wound of love, that through the opening of His side we may in return enter His Heart by means of love, and there be able to unite all our love with His divine love into one love, as the glowing iron is one with the fire. Therefore for the sake of this wound which Christ received for him on the Cross, when the dart of unconquerable love pierced His Heart, man should bring all his will into conformity with the will of God. But to fashion himself into conformity with Christ's sufferings, he should consider what surpassingly noble love our Lord has shown us in the opening of His side, since through it He has given us the wide open entrance into His Heart. Therefore, let man make haste to enter into the Heart of Christ: let him gather up all his love and unite it with the divine love."[8]

# Wisdom of the Saints

◆ St. Francis Xavier: "Every Christian should always be mindful of death and of the brevity of life, and of the exact accounting which he must render to God about his whole life past when he dies; and he should be mindful of the day of universal judgment, when we shall all arise in body and soul, and of the everlasting pains of hell, which will never end; and he should be mindful of the glory of paradise, for which we were created. If I think about these things each day, they will be a great help in disposing me to do now what I shall wish to have done at the hour of my death so that I may go to paradise."[9]

◆ St. Claude de la Columbière. In a letter the Saint writes:

"If I were in your place, this is how I would console myself. I would say to God with confidence: 'Lord, behold a soul who is in the world to exercise your admirable mercy, and to make it blaze out in the presence of heaven and earth. Others will glorify You in making visible the power of Your grace, by their fidelity and constancy, showing how sweet and generous You are to those who are faithful to You. For my part I will glorify You by making known how good You are to sinners, and that Your mercy is higher than all malice, that nothing can exhaust it, that no relapse, however shameful and guilty it may be, need cause a sinner to despair of pardon. I have grievously offended You, O my lovable Redeemer, but it would be worse still if I committed the horrible outrage against You of thinking that You were not kind enough to pardon.'"[10]

◆ St. John of the Cross, Doctor of the Church: "Strive to preserve your heart in peace and let no event of this world disturb it. Reflect that all must come to and end."[11]

"Take neither great nor little notice of who is with you or against you and try always to please God. Ask Him that His will be done in you. Love Him intensely, as He deserves to be loved."[12]

"Let your speech be such that no one may be offended, and let it concern things which would not cause you regret were all to know of them."[13]

◆ St. Therese of Lisieux: "This year, June 9, the feast of the Holy Trinity, I received the grace to understand more than ever before how much Jesus desires to be loved."[14]

"I understand so well that it is only love which makes us acceptable to God, that this love is the only good I ambition. Jesus deigned to show me the road that leads to this Divine Furnace, and this road is the surrender of the little child who sleeps without fear in its Father's arms."[15]

"Oh!, if all weak and imperfect souls felt what the least of souls feels, that is, the soul of your little Therese, not one would despair of reaching the summit of the mount of love. Jesus does not demand great actions from us but simply surrender and gratitude."[16]

"…He (Jesus) finds few hearts who surrender to Him without reservations, who understand the real tenderness of His infinite Love."[17]

"Neither do I desire any longer suffering or death, and still I love them both; it is love alone that attracts me, however. I desired them for a long time; I possessed suffering and believed I had touched the shores of heaven, that the little flower would be gathered in the springtime of her life. Now, abandonment alone guides me. I have no other compass! I can no longer ask for anything with fervor except the accomplishment of God's will in my soul without any creature being able to set obstacles in the way."[18]

◆ St. Teresa of Avila, Doctor of the Church: "How miserable is the wisdom of mortals and uncertain their providence! May You through Your providence, Lord, provide the necessary means by which my soul may serve You at Your pleasure rather than at its own."[19]

◆ St. Bernard, Doctor of the Church: "The first point to consider is that God deserves exceeding love from us, a love that has no measure. That is the first thing you must understand. The reason is, as I have said before, that He was first to love; He, Who is so great, loves us so much; He loves us freely, little and poor as we are. That is why I said in the beginning that the measure of our love for God is that there should be none. For since love given to God is given to the Infinite and Measureless, what measure or what limit could it have? And, what is more, our love is not bestowed for nothing, as is His; we render it in payment of a debt. He the Unmeasured and Eternal God, He Who is Love beyond all human ken. Whose greatness knows no bounds, Whose wisdom has no end, loves. Shall we, then, set a limit to our love for Him? I will love Thee, O Lord my Strength, my Strong Rock and my Defense, my Savior, my one Desire and Love. My God, my Helper, I will love Thee with all the power Thou hast given me; not worthily, for that can never be, but to the full of my capacity. Do what I will, I never can discharge my debt to Thee, and I can love Thee only according to the power that Thou has given me. But I will love Thee more and more, as Thou seest fit to give the further power; yet never, never, as Thou shouldst be loved. Thine eyes did see my substance, yet being imperfect; yet in Thy book are written all who do the best they can, though they can never pay their debt in full."[20]

◆ St. Peter Julian Eymard: "Our Lord Jesus Christ is our inheritance. He wants to give Himself to everybody, but not everybody wants Him. There are some who would want Him, but they will not submit to the condition of good and pure living which He has laid down; and their malice has the power to render God's bequest null and void."[21]

# Augustine and Trinitarian Spirituality

All authentic articulations of Christian spirituality are Trinitarian. Indeed, we go to the Father, through and with Christ, in the Holy Spirit, with the assistance of Mary our Mother. However, certain spiritualities highlight the Trinitarian framework of Christian spirituality more than do others. One of these is the spirituality of St. Augustine. Sr. Mary T. Clark, R.S.C.J., in commenting on Augustinian spirituality, observes: "Christ is the perfect image of the Father, equally God. The human person is an imperfect image of the Trinity, not equal to God but having a capacity for communion with God. The journey to God is by way of becoming a more perfect image of the divine Trinity. The Father's perfect image, his Son, is the only way to likeness with God. This likeness is best achieved through wisdom, the crowning gift of the Holy Spirit. Wisdom is 'the love and awareness of Him who is always present' (*Exposition*, Ps 135.8). On it depends the soul's loving intimacy with the divine Persons. It is the final fruit of a living faith that acts in love (see Gal 5:6). It presupposes an eager search for God, but its proper activity is contemplation, that is, the finding of God and rejoicing in Him.

"This indirect perception of God will become in heaven a direct face-to-face vision of God. The contemplation of God is the destiny of every Christian (*City of God*, 19.19). Here on earth wisdom expands into loving action. The Christian thereby acts out God's love for all creatures, just as Christ in His actions manifested God's love for them. The source of wisdom, the divine love poured into human hearts by the Spirit arouses in persons the acts of remembering, understanding, and loving God.

"Thus Augustine saw the essential process of the spiritual life to be the re-formation of the image of the Trinity in the human person by the grace of Christ freely accepted. Transformed into children of God, human persons enter into union with him not merely as creatures with Creator but as friends. The Father offers this grace of friendship to all through Christ, the universal way.

"So convinced was Augustine of the centrality of the Trinity in the living out of Christian faith that he wrote fifteen books on the Trinity…

"'We are certainly seeking a trinity, not any trinity at all, but that trinity which is God, the true, supreme, and only God…We are not yet speaking of heavenly things, not yet of God the Father, Son and Holy Spirit. Rather we speak of this unequal image, an image nevertheless, which is human being. For the mind's weakness perhaps looks upon this image with more familiarity and facility…Let us attend as much as we can and call upon the heavenly light to illuminate our darkness so that we might see, as much as we are permitted, the image of God in us' (*On the Trinity*, 9.1.1; 9.2.2). This human imaging of God is a call to authenticity, that is, to truth in word and action. The Son, the Word of God, was made flesh so that we might imitate Him in living rightly…"[22]

# The Church and the World

Fr. Robert Schwartz, a theologian and spiritual director at St. Paul's Seminary in St. Paul, MN., offers us these meaningful words on the Church and the world: "The church exists in the world, yet claims, as integral to its mission, an ultimate goal lying beyond the sphere of historical growth and human evolution. It participates in the human enterprise and contributes to the well-being of society while seeking completion in a realm which surpasses human creativity. The ecclesial community witnesses to human values at the same time that it locates the foundation of these values in a God who transcends history and material reality.

"The church is by definition a pilgrim, for its source of life and its goal transcend visible reality. Linked to the material world by human nature and by the very words and signs which mediate its life, the church seeks its true home in a kingdom which is yet to come. Although its members see temporal words and actions as important factors in attaining future beatitude, they do not propose themselves and their activity as the primary determinants of the kingdom nor earthly happiness as the fulfillment of human life."[23]

# The Priest as Shepherd

The theologian Jean Galot, S.J., has some insightful thoughts on the priest as shepherd: "As a mediator, the priest is a shepherd in the name of God, or more precisely, in the name of Christ, and through Christ, in the name of the Father. In the priest is realized the prophetic oracle of Ezechiel in which Yahweh promises to be the shepherd of his people (Ezek 34).

"Some implications of this principle must be underlined. The priest does not draw the inspiration for his pastoral zeal from his own feelings, from his own personal resolve to create a better world. He is shepherd on the strength of God's pastoral intention and represents specifically Christ the shepherd. Consequently, he is called upon to fulfill his pastoral mission not according to ideas of his own and his own personal ambitions, but in keeping with God's own dispensation and the design of salvation devised by the Father and carried out by Christ. Like Jesus himself, the priest is at the service of the Father."[24]

# On Prayer

Christian prayer is rooted in the personal relationship that exists between the Christian and the triune God. Prayer is becoming conscious, in a special way, of the fact that the life of grace brings us into a deeply intimate union with the divine Persons, a union that is so intimate that Father, Son and Holy Spirit actually dwell within us in the most personal fashion.

During prayer we are especially aware of God's presence to us and, reciprocally, of our presence to Him. This attitude of personal presence in love should dominate prayer. In prayer we are engaging in a love-dialogue with God who is so concerned with us. The personal presence of prayer should be rooted in our openness to God, in our willingness to listen to Him.

Being open to God in prayer, listening to Him, is based on the theological reality that God takes the initiative in the spiritual life. We never have to fear that God will fail to take the initiative. The danger lies with us, with the possibility that we will be deaf to God's call, that we will not listen properly, or that our openness to Him will be marred by our selfishness.

To be open to God in prayer means to listen to what He has to tell us about both Himself and ourselves. To be open to God in prayer means to be willing to allow God in His love to possess us more and more, to be willing to allow this love to direct our lives. To be open to God in prayer means a deepening desire to allow God's will to possess us entirely in Christ Jesus Our Lord.

---

We can be tempted to tell ourselves that we are too busy to pray. We are speaking about set, formal periods of prayer. We are not speaking about prayer in action or that prayerful attitude which should permeate our daily activity. This contemplation in action, far from distracting us from the proper attention we must give to duty, allows us to bring a deeper Christian awareness to what we are doing and why we are doing it.

In reference to formal, set periods of prayer, extremely busy schedules can lead us to tell ourselves that we don't have time for this kind of prayer— or at least not very often. If we say we don't have time to pray, something is wrong.

We cannot tell ourselves that we are busier than Jesus was, that we have more important work to accomplish than He did. Yet Scripture tells us that Jesus consistently set aside special times for prayer: "His reputation continued to grow, and large crowds would gather to hear him and to have their sickness cured, but he would always go off to some place where he could be alone and pray." (Lk 5:15-16). Many, many outstanding Christians of all states of life have likewise always found the time to pray. Moreover, they were more effective in their work precisely because they did pray.

Prayer helps us to be effective workers in various ways. Prayer helps us control worry and anxiety. Prayer has a significant contribution to offer in making us Christians who are basically permeated with the peace of Christ, who, because we realize what it means to be loved by Jesus, are in a position to control worry and anxiety. Prayer also aids us in our work and activity by giving us the motivation to do the right thing at the right time. Sometimes we can fail to do the work of the Lord precisely because we are not properly motivated. Prayer can also aid in making our work of a higher Christian quality—prayer can help permeate our work with a deeper faith, hope, and love. These are some of the ways prayer assists us to go about our work more efficiently. When we pause to analyze the situation, then, we have to admit that we are not too busy to pray. Indeed, we are too busy not to pray.

---

Thomas Merton tells us: "The contemplation of God in nature, which the Greek Fathers called *theoria physica,* has both a positive and a negative aspect. On the one hand, *theoria physica* is a positive recognition of God as he is manifested in the essences *(logoi)* of all things. It is not a speculative science of nature but rather a habit of religious awareness which endows the soul with a kind of intuitive perception of God as he is reflected in his creation. This instinctive religious view of things is not acquired by study so much as by ascetic detachment. And that implies that the positive and negative elements in this 'contemplation of nature' are really inseparable. The negative aspect of *theoria physica* is an equally instinctive realization of the vanity and illusion of all things as soon as they are considered apart from their right order and reference to God their Creator...

Does all this mean that the *theoria physica* of the Greek Fathers was a kind of perpetual dialectic between the two terms vision and illusion? No. In the Christian platonism of the Fathers, dialectic is no longer as important as it was in Plato and Plotinus. The Christian contemplation of nature does not consist in an intellectual tennis game between these two contrary aspects of nature. It consists rather in the ascetic gift of discernment which, in one penetrating glance, apprehends what creatures are, and what they are not. This is the intellectual counterpoise of detachment in the will. Discernment and detachment...are two characters of the mature Christian soul. They are not yet the mark of a mystic, but they bear witness that one is traveling the right way to mystical contemplation, and that the stage of beginners is passed."[25]

# Mary and the Priest

The *Directory of the Ministry and Life of Priests* tells us: "There is an 'essential rapport...between the Mother of Jesus and the priesthood of the ministry of the Son,' stemming from the existing one between the divine maternity of Mary and the priesthood of Christ.

"In light of such a rapport, Marian spirituality is rooted in every priest. Priestly spirituality could not be considered complete if it were to fail to include the message of Christ's words on the Cross, in which He conferred his Mother to the beloved disciple, and, through him, to all priests called to continue his work of redemption.

"Like John at the foot of the Cross, every priest has been entrusted, in a special way, with Mary as Mother (cf. Jn 19:26-27).

"Priests, who are among the favored disciples of Jesus, crucified and risen, should welcome Mary as their Mother in their own life, bestowing her with constant attention and prayer. The Blessed Virgin then becomes the Mother who leads them to Christ, who makes them sincerely love the Church, who intercedes for them and who guides them toward the Kingdom of heaven…

"But they are not devout sons if they do not know how to imitate the virtues of Mary. The priest will look to Mary to be a humble, obedient and chaste minister and to give testimony of charity in the total surrender to God and the Church".[26]

# Act of Consecration

Lord Jesus, Chief Shepherd of the Flock, I consecrate my priestly life to Your Heart, pierced on Calvary for love of us. From Your pierced Heart the Church was born, the Church You have called me, as a priest, to serve in a most special way. You reveal Your Heart as symbol of Your love in all its aspects, including Your most special love for me, whom You have chosen as Your priest-companion. Help me always to pour out my life in love of God and neighbor. Heart of Jesus, I place my trust in You!

Dear Blessed Virgin Mary, I consecrate myself to your maternal and Immaculate Heart, this Heart which is symbol of your life of love. You are the Mother of my Savior. You are also my Mother. You love me with the most special love as this unique priest-son. In a return of love I give myself entirely to your motherly love and protection. You followed Jesus perfectly. You are His first and perfect disciple. Teach me to imitate you in the putting on of Christ. Be my motherly intercessor so that, through your Immaculate Heart, I may be guided to an ever closer union with the pierced Heart of Jesus, Chief Shepherd of the Flock, Who leads me to the Father in the Holy Spirit.

# Letters

We thank all those who have taken the time to write to us. We very much appreciate your letters. Space limitations permit us to publish only a few of these.

It gives me special pleasure to share the following letter. It comes from my doctoral dissertation director, Fr. Ernie Larkin, O. Carm. He is one of the leading experts on the spiritual teaching of St. John of the Cross and St. Teresa of Avila. He has also been one of my most influential teachers, and for this I am most grateful to him.—*Editor*

Dear Ed,

I am embarrassed not to have been one of the first to congratulate you on your obviously successful newsletter for priests. It is...solid, inspirational, and founded in the best of our tradition. I am very proud of you. May the Lord touch many of our hearts through this ministry. All the best to you!

Ernie Larkin, O Carm.
Phoenix, Arizona

Dear Father Ed,

Prayer is truly the food of faith and faith is the foundation of our priestly lives. Through your Shepherds of Christ newsletter you remind us through your insights and prayers that emotion does indeed feed devotion and that we are all only a heartbeat away from the face-to-face presence of the Father through the Son in the Spirit!

Thanks for all your letter means to all of us.

Fraternally,
Msgr. Jeremiah F. Kenney
Baltimore, Maryland

Dear Father Ed,

The enclosed is a small way of thanking you for the articles in *Shepherds of Christ.*

The article "Thoughts on the Eucharist" (July-August) reminds me of the overwhelming love of Christ for me, fellow Catholics and the world. I pray in the vein of St. Peter Eymard that I might return my all and answer Christ with "this is me for you".

In Christ,
Fr. Joe Kenlon, O.F.M.Cap
New Paltz, New York

Dear Father Ed,

I must sincerely tell you how enjoyable your newsletter is. I find it spiritually uplifting. Many times in our earnestness to be of help we forget our own spiritual needs.

You are doing a great service to the American priesthood. May God bless you and sustain you in your endeavors. My prayers are with you, because I (and I am sure many other priests) feel enriched every time I read your newsletter.

Thanks.

In Jesus' love,
Rev. William Bonnici
Clinton Township, MI

## NOTES:

1. Scriptural quotations are taken from *The Jerusalem Bible,* Doubleday & Co.
2. Fr. Edward Leen, C.S.Sp., *The True Vine and Its Branches,* P.J. Kenedy & Sons, pp. 221 and 228.
3. Fr. Jordan Aumann, O.P., *Spiritual Theology,* Our Sunday Visitor, Inc., pp. 262-263.
4. Blessed Faustina Kowalska, *The Divine Mercy, Message and Devotion,* Marian Helpers, p. 27.
5. St. Claude de la Columbière, *An Act of Confidence in God,* Apostleship of Prayer, Chicago Regional Office.
6. St. Peter Julian Eymard, "The Most Blessed Sacrament Is Not Loved!," as in *The Treasury of Catholic Wisdom,* Fr. John Hardon, S.J., ed., Ignatius Press, p.584.
7. St. Bonaventure, "The Mystical Vine," Ch. 3, "Opera Omnia," Vol. VIII, as in *Heart of the Redeemer,* Timothy O'Donnell, Trinity Communications, p. 101.
8. Ludolph of Saxony, "The Life of Jesus Christ," as in *Heart of the Redeemer,* op. cit., pp. 112-113.
9. St. Francis Xavier, *Letters and Instructions of Francis Xavier,* Institute of Jesuit Sources, p. 207.
10. *Perfect Friend, Life of Claude de la Columbière,* B. Herder Book Company, p. 323.
11. *The Collected Works of St. John of the Cross,* translated by Kieran Kavanaugh, O.C.D., and Otilio Rodriguez, O.C.D., Doubleday and Company, "Maxims and Counsels", No. 75, p. 679.
12. Ibid., No. 76, p. 679.
13. Ibid., No. 72, p. 679.
14. *Story of a Soul, The Autobiography of St. Therese of Lisieux,* ICS Publications, p. 180.
15. Ibid., p. 188.
16. Ibid., p. 188.
17. Ibid., p. 189.
18. Ibid., p. 178.
19. *St. Teresa of Avila, Collected Works,* translated by Kieran Kavannaugh, O.C.D., and Otilio Rodriguez, O.C.D., ICS Publications, Vol. 1, "Soliloquies", No. 17, p. 462.
20. St. Bernard, "On the Love of God", as in *The Treasury of Catholic Wisdom,* op. cit., p. 189.
21. St. Peter Julian Eymard, "The Testament of Jesus Christ" as in *The Treasury of Catholic Wisdom,* op. cit., p. 573.
22. Sr. Mary T. Clark, R.S.C.J., in *The New Dictionary of Catholic Spirituality,* Michael Glazier, pp. 68-69.
23. Fr. Robert Schwartz, *Servant Leaders of the People of God,* Paulist Press, p. 91.
24. Fr. Jean Galot, S.J., *Theology of the Priesthood,* Ignatius Press, p. 144.
25. *The Ascent to the Truth,* Harcourt, Brace & Co., pp. 27-28.
26. "Directory on the Ministry and Life of Priests," No. 68, as in *Inside the Vatican,* special supplement, November, 1994, p.25.

A Publication of
Shepherds of Christ
Ministries

# shepherds of Christ

## A SPIRITUALITY NEWSLETTER FOR PRIESTS

NOVEMBER/DECEMBER 1995

Chief Shepherd of the Flock

# The Life of Prayer

"I am the good shepherd: the good shepherd is one who lays down his life for his sheep. The hired man, since he is not the shepherd and the sheep do not belong to him, abandons the sheep and runs away as soon as he sees a wolf coming, and then the wolf attacks and scatters the sheep. This is because he is only a hired man and has no concern for the sheep. I am the good shepherd. I know my own and my own know me, just as the Father knows me and I know the Father. And I lay down my life for my sheep." (Jn 10: 11 -15[1]).

Jesus was a man of deep prayer. The gospel of Luke tells us, "His reputation continued to grow, and large crowds would gather to hear him and to have their sickness cured, but he would always go off to some place where he could be alone and pray." (Lk 5:15-16).

See *The Life of Prayer,* page 95, top

## *Christmas Greetings*

At this Christmastime we wish all our readers a season filled with God's most special blessings. This season offers us a special occasion to reflect on these words:

"Yes, God loved the world so much that he gave his only Son, so that everyone who believes in him may not be lost but may have eternal life." (Jn 3:16).

May we who are priests respond to God's overwhelming love manifested in Christ Jesus Our Lord by feeding the Good Shepherd's flock with the food of love. Whether they sufficiently realize it or not, this is what they hunger for deep down—to realize how much Jesus loves them and to love Him in return.

#  Editor's Corner

by Edward Carter S.J.

Here in the U.S.A. we have recently celebrated Thanksgiving. Hopefully, at that time we all reminded ourselves that giving thanks to God is a daily duty.

A thankful person is a happy person. On occasions we experience sadness and unhappiness, perhaps one of the reasons is our failure to be properly thankful to God. Looking too much at what is wrong, we fail to be sufficiently aware of all that is right. We fail to realize sufficiently the many reasons we have to be joyful. Deficient in a spirit of thanksgiving, we also find ourselves deficient in a sense of joy.

Father, Son, and Holy Spirit have lavishly and lovingly given themselves to us—for this we need to be thankful. For the magnificent gift of the Eucharist—for this we need to be thankful. For Mary, for the Church, for our faith—these also call for our gratitude.

For life itself, for the opportunity to be and to become, to love and be loved, for the opportunity to accomplish the ordinary as well as the extraordinary, for the chance to grow and mature through both the painful and the exhilarating—for all this we need to be thankful.

For the preciousness of sight, for being able to hear the majestic symphonic sound as well as the gleeful laughter of children at play, for soundness of limb, for the general good health which accompanies us most of our days—for all this we owe perennial thanks.

For the wonderful people in our lives—for these we need to be thankful. Some of these have been very instrumental in helping us to be and to become what God destines us to be. Indeed, without them we may well not have grown in certain ways at all.

We should resolve to strive always to be appropriately thankful. We should endeavor consistently to be aware of the manifold and various gifts God abundantly bestows on us. We should resolve to maintain and develop that spirit of gratitude which will prevent Jesus from including us among the ungrateful, "As He entered one of the villages, ten lepers came to meet Him. They stood some way off and called to Him, 'Jesus! Master! Take pity on us.' When He saw them He said, 'Go and show yourselves to the priests.' Now as they were going away they were cleansed. Finding himself cured, one of them turned back praising God at the top of his voice and threw himself at the feet of Jesus and thanked Him. The man was a Samaritan. This made Jesus say, 'Were not all ten made clean? The other nine, where are they? It seems that no one has come back to give praise to God, except this foreigner.' And He said to the man, 'Stand up and go on your way. Your faith has saved you.'" (Lk 17:11-19).

*The Life of Prayer* continued from page 93

And in those hours immediately preceding His laying down His life for His sheep on the cross, He also prayed, "'My Father,' he said, 'if it is possible, let this cup pass me by. Nevertheless, let it be as you, not I, would have it.'" (Mt 26:39).

We, as priests of the Chief Shepherd, Jesus, are also called to lay down our lives for the flock. Relatively few priests throughout the Church's history have been called to shed their blood for the flock through physical martyrdom. All, though, have been and are called to lay down their lives in that spiritual martyrdom which is involved in giving oneself in loving service to the flock according to the Father's will.

To do this day after day as we should—pour out our lives in love of God and others—is impossible without a consistent prayer life.

We are effective shepherds to the extent we are united with Christ in love. And our growing union with Christ depends mightily on a life of consistent prayer.

# Thoughts on Prayer

◆ **Monastic Prayer.** Fr. Basil Pennington, O.C.S.O., the well-known spiritual writer, speaks to us about monastic life and prayer. We who are not monks can appropriately adapt what he says to our own spiritual lives:

"Those who embrace the monastic life want to follow Christ and to live the Christian life to the full. This they do with particular attention to the hidden life of Jesus, recognizing his own call to periods of solitude and mindful of his practice of going apart in order to pray. Jesus' years of growth were so hidden that we know little of them, but as a member of a devout Jewish family, it is likely that it was his practice to give time to prayer on a regular basis. After his baptism by John in the Jordan, he went into the desert for weeks of solitude, silence, and prayer (Mk 1:11-13). As the busy years of his healing ministry unfolded, he went apart again and again, alone or with his chosen friends, to pray (Mt 14:13; 14:23; 17:1; 20:17; Mk 6:30)."[2]

◆ **Prayer and Self-Identity.** There is a connection between prayer and growth in self-identity. In prayer, there is a greater grasp of who I am—this unique person that God has created and redeemed—and how God wants me to act.

In the quiet of prayer, we have the opportunity to gather up what would otherwise become the fragmented, disintegrated pieces of our lives. Prayer is meant to be a constructive and integrative force that will help us delineate

more clearly our self-identity. Through the light of prayer, we see how the
pieces fit together, how the Christlike self in its uniqueness is meant to give
shape and meaning to all facets of our existence.

During prayer, the Spirit gives not only the light that allows us to grow in
awareness of the Christlike self, but also the determination to act upon this
awareness. The Spirit gives us the strength to allow the Christlike self to
increasingly unfold in and through all dimensions of our existence. We thus
grow in union with Christ, this Christ who desires
to lead us ever closer to the Father in the Holy
Spirit.

◆ At times, we suffer during prayer because
God seems far away. We long for a closer union
with Him, but there almost seems to be a wall
between God and us. When this happens, we
should examine ourselves to see if there is an obvious and significant deficiency in our present
Christian existence. Is there something that we are
doing and should not be doing, or something that
we should be doing and are not? If such an exami-
nation uncovers no significant deficiency, we can be reasonably assured that
this seeming absence of God is one of the pains that we can sometimes
encounter during prayer's positive, evolving journey. We must also remember, as the lives of mystics remind us, that God can be very close to us precisely at those times when He seems far away.

◆ There is a definite pain experienced during prayer's transformation of
consciousness as one goes from an awareness of the false self to a growing
awareness of the true, Christlike self. To cut through the layers of pride, selfishness, greed, laziness, hedonism, and so on, that blemish the pristine
image of the Christlike self is no painless task. Cooperating with prayer's
illumination, which points out those ugly manifestations of the false self,
carries with it its own kind of pain. Likewise, cooperating with prayer's
strength in order to correct these manifestations of the false self requires a
willingness to suffer.

As we cut through the layers of the false self and descend more and more
to the vibrant and refreshing realms of the Christlike self, we are also open
to the pain that accompanies a certain type of fear. During prayer, as we
become more aware of both the Christlike self and what the Christlike self
demands, we can become afraid. We know this Christlike self longs for a
greater love union with God, but we fear what this will demand of us. We
hesitate. We want to say a full yes to God's love, but we may find this very
difficult to do.

We waver, torn between the inexorable desire to come closer to God and the dread which is born of the realization of the cost that is involved. This suspended state can, indeed, be very painful. We must come to realize that the pain of the wavering, the pain of the suspended condition, is greater than is the suffering involved in giving God what He wants.

◆ Some say that prayer is a risk, that the one who prays is opening himself or herself to what God asks during prayer, and what God asks might be difficult and contrary to one's own plans and ideas. If prayer is a risk, it is a risk for happiness. Sometimes we try to pursue happiness apart from God's design. If we are honest with ourselves, we must admit that such a path is strewn with frustration and disappointment, and is dead-ended. True happiness is never possible apart from God's will for us, and we know this. Why, then, do we not live this truth with the fullness of our being? Giving God what He asks in prayer always results in greater happiness.

◆ At times we can feel we are engaged in superficial living, that we are, in a sense, merely gliding along on the surface of life. We may not be terribly unhappy, but we tell ourselves in moments of honesty that there must be more to life than what we are experiencing. Such whisperings of conscience are a cry for the deep, meaningful, and fulfilling type of existence that God intends for us. One of the reasons we can become mired in the mediocrity of superficial living is our failure to pray as we should.

◆ Pope John Paul II observes: "Much has been written about prayer, and further, prayer has been widely experienced in the history of humankind, especially in the history of Israel and Christianity. Man achieves *the fullness of prayer…when he lets God be most fully present in prayer. The history of mystical prayer* in the East and West attests to this: Saint Francis, Saint Teresa of Avila, Saint John of the Cross, Saint Ignatius of Loyola, and in the East, for example, Saint Serafim of Sarov and many others."[3]

◆ Pope Paul VI on the rosary: "As a Gospel prayer, centered in the mystery of the redemptive Incarnation, the Rosary is therefore a prayer with a clearly Christological orientation—the Jesus that each Hail Mary recalls is the same Jesus Whom the succession of the mysteries proposes to us…By its nature the recitation of the Rosary calls for a quiet rhythm and a lingering pace, helping the individual to meditate on the mysteries of the Lord's life as seen through the eyes of her who was closest to the Lord. In this way the unfathomable riches of these mysteries are unfolded."[4]

◆ A well-known spiritual writer of our times, Dom Hubert Van Zeller, offers us thoughts concerning prayer and the burden of everydayness: "When asked what he considered to be the most exacting aspect of the religious life, a certain experienced superior replied without a moment's hesitation: 'Staying on the job.' This can be taken to apply to the spiritual as well as to the monastic life. It signifies more than the determination not to bolt. Though it bears first upon obedience and perseverance, staying on the job knows such refinements as patience in the face of panic, endurance of doubt, silent submission when misjudged, suppression of criticism and ambition, continuance in the drudgery of uncongenial and unrewarding work…the fight against resentment and self-pity…If staying on the job demands a measure of heroism, it certainly demands a resolute unselfishness. Even in those who are not (for want of a better term) imaginative, and to whom routine occupations are no great burden, the spirit of rebellion will assert itself occasionally, and there will be a longing for rest, change…

"There must be very few people in the world who positively like monotony. Yet because so much of life is drearily monotonous, those who were looking to serve God with their lives must accustom themselves to dull, steady daily labors, and make of them an acceptable sacrifice. This can be done effectively only by staying with the interior job of prayer. It is stability in prayer which brings order and stability to outward occupations."[5]

♦ The Curé of Ars, St. John Vianney, has some very direct words for us priests concerning prayer: "What keeps us priests back from the attainment of holiness is lack of consideration. It displeases us to withdraw our minds from outside things. We do not know what we rightly do. We have need of intimate reflection, continuous prayer and intimate union with God."[6]

♦ A modern master on prayer, Thomas Merton, offers us some sobering thoughts: "And so, many contemplatives never become great saints, never enter into close friendship with God, never find a deep participation in His immense joys, because they cling to the miserable little consolations that are given to beginners in the contemplative way.

"How many there are who are in a worse state still: they never even get as far as contemplation because they are attached to activities and enterprises that seem to them to be important. Blinded by their desire for ceaseless motion, for a constant sense of achievement, famished with a crude hunger for results, for visible and tangible success, they work themselves into a state in which they cannot believe they are pleasing God unless they are busy with a dozen jobs at the same time. Sometimes they fill the air with lamentations and complain that they no longer have any time for prayer, but they have become such experts in deceiving themselves that they do not realize how insincere their lamentations are. They not only allow themselves to be involved in more and more work, they actually go looking for new jobs. And the busier they become the more mistakes they make. Accidents and errors pile up all around them. They will not be warned. They go further and further from the shore—and then perhaps God allows their mistakes to catch up with them. Then they wake up and discover that their carelessness has involved them in some gross and obvious sin against justice, for instance, or against the obligations of their state."[7]

♦ Our proper Eucharistic participation demands a thorough preparation.

It is preparation which we must be willing to achieve all day, every day. This preparation includes the practice of prayer, especially that based on the mysteries of Christ's life, death, and resurrection. This prayer helps one to approach the Mass with the mind of Christ, enabling one to more vitally assimilate the mysteries of Christ which the liturgy makes sacramentally present.

And as we participate in the Mass, we should be aware, of course, that the Eucharist itself is the greatest prayer.

◆ One of the most eminent theologians of our times, Hans Urs Von Balthasar, says: "Those who consider Christian contemplation outdated and turn to the values of the world to give them fresh force are victims of an illusion. Only 'in Christ' do things attain their ultimate meaning and end..."[8]

◆ The Father, in the Holy Spirit, speaks to the Christian in prayer through Christ. The Father, under the delicate touches of the Spirit, enlightens the Christian as to life's meaning. Just as all creation must seek its ultimate meaning in Christ, so the individual Christian can only really understand his or her existence in the light of Christ.

Because of the central role of Christ in the act of prayer, certain corollaries follow. Our prayer should be rooted in Christ and His Gospel. We should make no deliberate attempts on our own in prayer to withdraw from the thought of Christ in His humanity, as if the thought of this sacred humanity is an obstacle to higher prayer. This was an error in the quietism of Molinos. This error, in various degrees, has also been found in the teachings of others besides Molinos, although perhaps not as boldly. St. Teresa of Avila, an outstanding teacher on prayer, was exposed to this error and has pointed out its dangers: "How much more is it necessary not to withdraw through one's own efforts from all our good and help which is the most sacred humanity of our Lord Jesus Christ. I cannot believe that these souls do so, but they just don't understand; and they will do harm to themselves and to others."[9]

# Thoughts on the Eucharist

Our greatest prayer is the Eucharist. Here are some thoughts on this great Gift of Jesus to us:

It is within the Mass, the heart of the liturgy, that the Christian meets Christ and His mysteries in a most special way. In faith, hope, and love the Christian is in union with Jesus in the most intimate fashion, and receives the graces necessary for growth into an ever greater likeness to Christ. Through the graces of the Eucharist, the Christian is enabled to relive the mysteries of Christ's life, death, and resurrection in his or her own life. How true it is to say that the liturgy, centered in the Mass, is aimed at transformation in Christ.

◆ Henri Nouwen observes, "The tragedy is that much resentment is hidden within the Church. It is one of the most paralyzing aspects of the Christian community.

"Still, the Eucharist presents another option. It is the possibility to choose not resentment, but gratitude. Mourning our losses is the first step away from resentment and toward gratitude. The tears of our own grief can soften our hardened hearts and open us to the possibility to say 'thanks'.

"The word 'Eucharist' means literally 'act of thanksgiving'. To celebrate the Eucharist and to live a Eucharistic life has everything to do with gratitude. Living Eucharistically is living life as a gift, a gift for which one is grateful."[10]

# Three Great Teachers on Prayer

St. John of the Cross, St. Teresa of Avila, and St. Ignatius Loyola have all three spoken eloquently on the subject of prayer. Fr. Thomas McKenna, C.M., offers some insightful observations concerning their spiritual doctrine: "Confessing that the approach to God happens only on God's terms, Teresa nonetheless painted the way there in warm and welcoming colors. Her chronicle of the journey through a series of successively enclosed chambers (mansions) is classic among the descriptions of the mystical path. Sparkling as it does with images of emerging butterflies and bubbling artesian wells, it depicts her move from active to passive contemplation. Hardly a passive personality, Teresa initiated a prodigious reform within the Carmelites and thus also testified to the synergy between genuine interior life and effective apostolic action.

"If Teresa sketched resting points along the spiritual ascent, her protegé, John of the Cross, fixed his gaze on the summit. Compactly in his poetry but also in interpretive prose, John detailed the melting-down and recasting of human desire as it draws near the Divine. His is a shadowy passage through a twilight of the senses and spirit, an intensely dark nocturne, and out into a dawn streaked with the divine light. Over the course of that night, the darkness that blinded the traveler is revealed as the radiance of God, which at the earlier stage could not be recognized for the light it was...

"Ignatius of Loyola took a different tack as he found intimacy with God in the press of active service. As he interacted with his times and circumstances, he discovered certain patterns of divine guidance embedded within his experience and subsequently constructed an imaginatively rich method to help others appropriate theirs. Basic to his logic was a conviction that the Spirit of Jesus is 'afoot in the universe,' particularly within each individual, and that therefore the Spirit-filled person is able to know by both interior and exterior signs which activities are the genuine works of Christ. Such a mystical perception of the world ties the closest of bonds between prayer and ministry, prodding the apostle to view all activities in their relation to their divine ground, and conversely to find that source in all things."[11]

# Prayer to the Good Shepherd

St. Gregory of Nyssa has left us this inspiring prayer to the Good Shepherd:

"Where do you pasture your sheep, O Good Shepherd, you who carry on your shoulders the whole flock? For it is but one sheep, this entire human race whom you lift onto your shoulders. Show me the place where there are green pastures, let me know restful waters, lead me out to nourishing grass and call me by name so that I can hear your voice, for I am your sheep. And through that voice calling me, give me eternal life.

"Tell me, you whom my soul loves. This is how I address you, because your true name is above all other names; it is unutterable and incomprehensible to all rational creatures. And so the name I use for you is simply the statement of my soul's love for you, and this is an apt name for making your goodness known. Very dark though I am, how could I not love you who so loved me that you laid down your life for the sheep you tend? No greater love can be conceived than this, that you should purchase my salvation at the cost of your life."[12]

# On Suffering

In God's plan, suffering is meant to lead to greater life. God tells us this with absolute clarity as we look at Jesus, the Suffering Servant. The cross of Jesus was not an end in itself, but a means to greater life for the whole human race. Our own sufferings can either be wasted or used to achieve greater life for ourselves and others. Dom Hubert Van Zeller observes: "Men and women who might be turning their afflictions over to God, who have only to unite themselves in spirit with Christ's passion, are found so often to stop short, and even to make of their trial further matter for selfishness. Even if we do not rebel positively against God's providential will, we can become so preoccupied with our troubles as to leave God out of account.

"Instead of making us compassionate for others we can squander compassion on ourselves. Suffering is meant to enlarge our hearts, not shrink them. With suffering goes the grace of patience, peace, fortitude, penitence and love. All this can be missed if we make the mistake of turning in upon ourselves as the result of our trials.

"To the Jews the cross was a stumbling-block, and to the gentiles foolishness. What is it to us? Often it can be an emblem merely, the significance of the symbol forgotten. The cross is something in which we are, by reason of our Christian inheritance, inextricably involved. Do we yield to it or harden ourselves against it? The cross is not just two planks fitted together on a certain day in the history of the world, and of all the relics which we venerate the most sacred, but a fact of our human experience which may or may not be sacred according to what we do about it."[13]

To suffer properly, to use suffering according to God's will and thereby grow through it, demands that we be persons of prayer. The light which God gives us in prayer helps us to see the purpose of suffering in His plan. The strength given to us in prayer helps us to live accordingly.

# The Priest as Shepherd

Vatican II tells us: "By their vocations and ordination, priests of the New Testament are indeed set apart in a certain sense within the midst of God's people. But this is so, not that they may be separated from the people or from any man, but that they may be totally dedicated to the work for which the Lord has raised them up. They cannot be ministers of Christ unless they are witnesses and dispensers of a life other than this earthly one. But they cannot be of service to men if they remain strangers to the life and conditions of men. Their ministry itself by a special title forbids them to be conformed to this world. Yet at the same time this ministry requires that they live in this world among men, and that as good shepherds they know their sheep. It requires that they seek to lead those who are not of this sheepfold so that they too may hear the voice of Christ and that there may be one fold and one Shepherd."[14]

# Pope John Paul II in the USA

Here are some excerpts from the many remarks made by the Holy Father during his recent visit to the United States:

♦ "The right to life is the first of all rights. It is the foundation of democratic liberties and the keystone of the edifice of civil society. Both as Americans and as followers of Christ, American Catholics must be committed to the defense of life in all its stages and in every condition."

♦ "America's sometimes extravagant affluence often conceals much hardship and poverty. We must therefore ask a very basic question: have the people living in this huge metropolis lost sight of the blessings which belong to the poor in spirit?"

♦ "You are called to stand up for life! To respect and defend the mystery of life always and everywhere...Stand up for the life of the aged and handicapped, against attempts to promote assisted suicide and euthanasia! Stand up for marriage and family life! Stand up for purity!"

♦ "The family is placed at the center of the great struggle between life and death, between love and all that is opposed to love. The family therefore is at the heart of the Church's mission and of her concern for humanity."

♦ "Every generation of Americans needs to know that freedom consists not in doing what we like, but in having the right to do what we ought."

♦ "I speak of your founding documents: the Declaration of Independence, the Constitution, the Bill of Rights—and I say to you again, America, in the light of your own traditions: love life, cherish life, defend life, from conception to natural grave."[15]

# The Christian and the Social Order

Vatican II tells us: "Coming down to practical and particularly urgent consequences, this council lays stress on reverence for man; everyone must consider his every neighbor without exception as another self, taking into account first of all his life and the means necessary to living it with dignity, so as not to imitate the rich man who had no concern for the poor man Lazarus.

"In our times a special obligation binds us to make ourselves the neighbor of absolutely every person, and of actively helping him when he comes across our path, whether he be an old person abandoned by all, a foreign laborer unjustly looked down upon, a refugee, a child born of an unlawful union and wrongfully suffering for a sin he did not commit, or a hungry person...

"Furthermore, whatever is opposed to life itself, such as any type of murder, genocide, abortion, euthanasia, or willful self-destruction; whatever violates the integrity of the human person, such as mutilation, torments inflicted on body or mind, attempts to coerce the will itself; whatever insults human dignity, such as subhuman living conditions, arbitrary imprisonment, deportation, slavery, prostitution, the selling of women and children; as well as disgraceful working conditions, where men are treated as mere tools for profit, rather than as free and responsible persons;

all these things and others of their like are infamies indeed. They poison human society, but they do more harm to those who practice them than those who suffer from the injury. Moreover, they are a supreme dishonor to the Creator."[16]

# On Non-Violence

Martin Luther King, Jr., has left us these words: "The nonviolent approach does not immediately change the heart of the oppressor. It first does something to the hearts and souls of those committed to it. It gives them a new self-respect; it calls up resources of strength and courage that they did not know they had. Finally, it reaches the opponent and so stirs his conscience that reconciliation becomes a reality."[17]

# Act of Consecration

Lord Jesus, Chief Shepherd of the Flock, I consecrate my priestly life to Your Heart, pierced on Calvary for love of us. From Your pierced Heart the Church was born, the Church You have called me, as a priest, to serve in a most special way. You reveal Your Heart as symbol of Your love in all its aspects, including Your most special love for me, whom You have chosen as Your priest-companion. Help me always to pour out my life in love of God and neighbor. Heart of Jesus, I place my trust in You!

Dear Blessed Virgin Mary, I consecrate myself to your maternal and Immaculate Heart, this Heart which is symbol of your life of love. You are the Mother of my Savior. You are also my Mother. You love me with the most special love as this unique priest-son. In a return of love I give myself entirely to your motherly love and protection. You followed Jesus perfectly. You are His first and perfect disciple. Teach me to imitate you in the putting on of Christ. Be my motherly intercessor so that, through your Immaculate Heart, I may be guided to an ever closer union with the pierced Heart of Jesus, Chief Shepherd of the Flock, Who leads me to the Father in the Holy Spirit.

# The Holy Spirit in Our Lives

As the closing words of the act of consecration remind us, Jesus leads us to the Father in the Holy Spirit with Mary at our side. The Holy Spirit desires to fashion us into an ever greater likeness of Christ according to Jesus' pattern of death-resurrection. Mary our Mother cooperates with the Spirit, Whose spouse she is, in this process. Obviously, we should pray to the Holy Spirit each day. There are many ways we can do this. We can do this by simply turning our attention to the Spirit at various times during the day as we ask for His guidance. This method can also be complemented by saying certain established prayers. Here is one of these: "Come Holy Spirit, Almighty Sanctifier. God of love, Who filled the Virgin Mary with grace, Who wonderfully changed the hearts of the apostles, Who endowed all your martyrs with marvelous courage, come and sanctify us. Enlighten our minds, rectify our judgment, set our hearts on fire, and preserve us from the misfortunes of resisting Your inspirations. Amen."

# Letters

We thank all those who have taken the time to write to us. We very much appreciate your letters. Space limitations permit us to publish only a few of these.

Dear Fr. Ed,

Thanks for the Shepherds of Christ newsletter. I enjoyed the July-August one. 'Twas very good and uplifting. May the Holy Spirit pierce your mind with ways to encourage your brother priests.

Fraternally in Christ,
Rev. John Turk
Warren, Ohio

Dear Father Ed,

With all the misquotes and the twisted interpretations of the Catholic Teachings in our daily Press, it is enjoyable to pick up Shepherds of Christ and read some solid Catholic Teaching. Keep up the good work.

Thank you for the Newsletter.

Fr. Werner Verhoff, C.PP.S.

Dear Fr. Carter,

I appreciated very much that you wrote to me. I can imagine the amount of work you have in publishing a newsletter for 45,000 priests and preparing to send it to priests in other countries. I congratulate you that you send it free of charge...

I received only two issues. I would love to get every issue. Your newsletter is a mine of thoughts and inspirations...

...in my humble opinion, encouragement is what priests need the most today. Everybody should show them their appreciation...for bearing the burdens of those who left or are not coming. I admire the great majority of young priests for their beautiful spirituality.

Yours respectfully in the Sacred Hearts of Jesus and Mary,
Fr. Leonard Currieri, M.SS.CC.
Linwood, New Jersey

Dear Ed,

In the true spirit of St. Ignio you have captured the essence of some very great saints in the Church. I found your selections truly inspiring and reinforcing of the beliefs that must be at the center of every priest's life. Thank you and keep up this long needed newsletter.

Father Jim Wysocki,
Marine City, Michigan

NOTES:

1. Scriptural quotations are taken from *The Jerusalem Bible*, Doubleday & Co.
2. Basil Pennington, O.C.S.O., as in *The New Dictionary of Catholic Spirituality*, The Liturgical Press, pp. 665-666.
3. Pope John Paul II, *Crossing the Threshold of Hope*, Alfred A. Knopp. p. 18.
4. Pope Paul VI, *Devotion to the Blessed Virgin Mary (Marialis Cultus)*, United States Catholic Conference, Nos. 46-47.
5. Dom Hubert Van Zeller, *More Ideas for Prayer*, Templegate, p. 112.
6. Pope John XXIII, *The Curè of Ars and the Priesthood*, Encyclical Letter, Paulist Press, p. 16.
7. Thomas Merton, *Seeds of Contemplation*, New Directions, pp. 127-128.
8. Hans Urs Von Balthasar, *Prayer*, Sheed & Ward. p. 53.
9. St. Teresa of Avila, "The Interior Castle," Bk. VI, Ch. 7, as in *The Collected Works of St. Teresa of Avila*, tr., Kiernan Kavanaugh, O.C.D., and Otilio Rodriguez, O.C.D., ICS Publications, Vol II, p. 399.
10. Henri Nouwen, *With Burning Hearts*, Orbis, p. 30.
11. Thomas McKenna, C.M., as in *The New Dictionary of Catholic Spirituality*, The Liturgical Press, p. 662.
12. St. Gregory of Nyssa, as in *The Liturgy of the Hours*, Catholic Book Publishing Co., Vol. IV, p. 555.
13. Dom Hubert Van Zeller, op. cit., p. 91.
14. "Decree on the Ministry and Life of Priests," *The Documents of Vatican II*, America Press, No. 3.
15. Pope John Paul II, as in *Inside the Vatican*, November, 1995.
16. "The Church in the Modern World," Vatican II, op. cit., #27.
17. Martin Luther King, Jr. as in *The Mystic Vision*, compiled by Andrew Harvey and Anne Baring, Harper, p. 168.

A Publication of
Shepherds of Christ
Ministries

# shepherds of Christ

## A SPIRITUALITY NEWSLETTER FOR PRIESTS

JANUARY/FEBRUARY 1998

Chief Shepherd of the Flock

# Our Life in Christ

"I am the good shepherd: the good shepherd is one who lays down his life for his sheep. The hired man, since he is not the shepherd and the sheep do not belong to him, abandons the sheep and runs away as soon as he sees a wolf coming, and then the wolf attacks and scatters the sheep. This is because he is only a hired man and has no concern for the sheep. I am the good shepherd. I know my own and my own know me, just as the Father knows me and I know the Father. And I lay down my life for my sheep." (Jn 10:11-15[1]).

Yes, the Good Shepherd has laid down His life for us. Through His life, His brutal and agonizing death on the cross, and His glorious resurrection, He has achieved new life for us. We truly live a new life in Christ Jesus, Our Lord. St. Paul tells us: "You have been taught that when we were baptized in Christ Jesus we were baptized in His death: In other words, when we were baptized we went into the tomb with Him and joined Him in death, so that as Christ was raised from the dead by the Father's glory, we too might live a new life." (Rom 6: 3-4).

And again Paul speaks to us: "...wherever we may be, we carry with us in our body the death of Jesus, so that the life of Jesus, too, may always be seen in our body." (2 Cor 4:10).

Christ has come to give us a share in Trinitarian life. In Baptism the Persons of the Trinity have given themselves to us in an extraordinary fashion. The intimacy of this Trinitarian communication imprints upon us the image of the Trinity. Because Christ as man mediates this Trinitarian gift, this image also possesses a Christlike dimension. This Christlike, Trinitarian image within us is our life of sanctifying grace. This life of grace, this Christ-life, allows us to communicate with Father, Son and Holy Spirit, the divine Persons who dwell within us. This Christ-life allows us to pour ourselves out in love of God and neighbor.

The life that Christ has given us is not a type of superstructure which is erected atop our human nature. Although nature and grace are distinct, they are not side by side as separate entities. Rather, grace permeates nature.

See *Our Life in Christ,* page 109, top

# Editor's Corner

by Edward Carter S.J.

We live in very critical times. The Church and the world are facing some of the most challenging problems ever.

We see a mixed picture as we look upon today's world. On the one hand, immorality is extremely pervasive. There are 50 million abortions performed across the world each year. Violence, in various forms, seems to have reached unprecedented proportions. Sexual promiscuity is rampant. Various injustices against the most helpless and marginalized peoples of the world seem more widespread than ever. The deterioration of many marriages and families is a stark reality. And, underlying all this, is a degree of atheism, agnosticism, and religious indifference which seems to be greater than at any time in history. To admit to all of the above is not to be pessimistic, but realistic.

On the other hand, God is forming many saintly people in all walks of life to counterbalance the widespread evil in the world. An example of this is that interest in spirituality on the part of a significant portion of the laity could well be at an all-time peak.

The quest for holiness on the part of many, then, is a reality, and seemingly on the increase. This desire for growth in holiness will, I believe, soon help lead the Church and the world into a great new era of peace in which love for God and neighbor will dominate the world.

We priests have the awesome privilege and responsibility to lead the flock in the quest for holiness. And what is holiness? We all know the answer. It is union with Jesus, it is the living of the Christ-life. Growth in holiness is becoming more aware of how much Jesus loves each one of us and increasingly responding with our own gift of self in love to our magnificent Savior, the One Who loves so tremendously, the One Who desires to lead us even closer to the Father in the Holy Spirit.

If we priests are to lead the flock in the quest for growth in holiness, surely we ourselves must have a consistent desire to grow in holiness, a consistent desire to utilize those means which God puts before us for developing our life in Christ. By his reception of the Sacrament of Holy Orders, the priest is meant to apply to himself in a special way the words of St. Paul in his Second Letter to Timothy: "So you are never to be ashamed of witnessing to the Lord, or ashamed of me for being his prisoner; but with me, bear the hardships for the sake of the Good News, relying on the power of God who has saved us and called us to be holy—not because of anything we ourselves have done but for his own purpose and by his own grace. This grace had already been granted to us, in Christ Jesus, before the beginning of time, but it has only been revealed by the appearing of our Savior Christ Jesus." (2 Tim 1:8-10).

---

*Our Life in Christ* continued from page 107

The Christian is one graced person. He or she has been raised up into a deeper form of life in Christ Jesus. Nothing that is authentically human has been excluded from the new existence. Whatever is really human in the life of the Christian is meant to be an expression of the Christ-life. The simple but deep joys of family life, the warm embrace of a mother for her child, the joy of being accepted by another in deep friendship, the wonderment at nature's beauty, the agony of crucial-decision making, the success or frustration that is experienced in one's work, the joy of being well received by others and the heartache of being misunderstood—all these human experiences are intended to be caught up in Christ and made more deeply human because of Him.

Christ, has come, then, not to destroy anything which is authentically human, but to perfect it by leading it to a graced fulfillment.

# Reflections on the Christ-life

◆ As I live the Christ-life, I should ask for a growing realization of how much Jesus loves me as this unique person. Jesus suffered and died for the entire human race, but He did it in a manner which makes it true to say He also did it for each individual in a most special way. Notice how personalized St. Paul makes the redemptive suffering and death and love of Jesus. In the Letter to the Galatians he does not use the plural, but the singular: "I have been crucified with Christ, and I live now not with my own life but with the life of Christ who lives in me. The life I now live in this body I live in faith: faith in the Son of God who loved me and who sacrificed himself for my sake." (Gal 2: 19-20).

◆ And Fr. Joseph Chorpenning, O.S.F.S., writing on the spirituality of Francis de Sales, saint and doctor of the Church, reminds us: "In human relationships one seeks to awaken in others an awareness of their divine dignity by the respect and reverence one demonstrates for their person, individuality, and liberty. For example, Francis says that when Jesus accomplished our redemption on the day of His passion and death, 'He knew all of us by name and by surname.'"[2]

◆ Jesus tells us to lose ourselves in Him, that it is only in Him that we can achieve His command of love. He tells us that love is the key. He tells us that the more we realize His great, individualized love for each of us, the more His plan for us becomes clear. His plan for us is summed up in His command to love God and to love our neighbor as ourselves. And He tells us that He is the source of our capacity to love.

◆ In a previous issue we quoted from a book by one of our readers, Msgr. Bob Guste. Because his thoughts are so appropriate regarding our present topic, we repeat part of the quotation: "Ideal Catholics held up to us by the Church are the saints. As you read their lives, what do you notice? One after the other, they were men and women who had a deep, personal relationship with Our Lord Jesus Christ. Their hearts were on fire with love for Him…

"Sometimes for us Catholics, when we read these lines or hear them, we think 'well, that was okay for them but it's not for me!' The Church honors them in order to say, 'Hey! It is for you!' We're all called to genuine holiness, as the Second Vatican Council reminds us. We're all called to grow every day in knowing, loving and serving Our Lord Jesus Christ. That's our goal, and everything we do in the Church is meant to foster that goal."[3]

◆ Fulgentius of Ruspe, Bishop, says: "Notice, at the conclusion of our prayer we never say 'through the Holy Spirit,' but rather, 'through Jesus Christ, your Son, our Lord.' Through the mystery of the Incarnation, Jesus Christ *became man, the mediator of God and man. He is a priest forever according to the order of Melchizedek. By shedding His own blood He entered once and for all into the Holy Places. He did not enter a place made by human hands, a mere type of the true one;* but He entered heaven itself, where He is at God's right hand interceding for us. Quite correctly, the church continues to reflect this mystery in her prayer…"

"We do not, however, only say 'your Son' when (we) conclude our prayer. We also say, 'who lives and reigns with you in the unity of the Holy Spirit.' In this way we commemorate the natural unity of the Father, Son and Holy Spirit. It is clear, then, that the Christ who exercises a priestly role on our behalf is the same Christ who enjoys a natural unity and equality with the Father and the Holy Spirit."[4]

◆ A leading representative of the French School of Spirituality, St. John Eudes says: "I ask you to consider that our Lord Jesus Christ is your true head and that you are a member of His body.

He belongs to you as the head belongs to the body. All that is His is yours: breath, heart, body, soul and all His faculties. All these you must use as if they belonged to you, so that in serving Him you may give Him praise, love and glory. You belong to Him as a member belongs to the head. This is why He earnestly desires you to serve and glorify the Father by using all your faculties as if they were His."[5]

◆ Speaking of the French School of Spirituality, Fr. Lowell Glendon, S.S. says: "While Christianity, by its very nature, is in some manner centered on

Christ, the French School has its own way of expressing and living this truth. Christ is seen as the incarnate Word, the one who offers perfect religion, i.e., praise, adoration, obedience, and love to God. Therefore we are called to conform ourselves to Jesus Christ, especially in His "states"…, i.e., the interior dispositions through which He faithfully lived out the mysteries of His incarnation, passion, death, resurrection and ascension."[6]

◆ Fr. Henri Nouwen has been one of the most influential spiritual writers of our times. His following words emphasize the overwhelming importance of the Christian leader's being intimately united with Jesus—and as priests we are certainly called to be leaders.

"Christian leaders cannot simply be persons who have well-informed opinions about the burning issues of our times. Their leadership must be rooted in the permanent intimate relationship with the incarnate Word, Jesus, and they need to find there the source for their words, advice and guidance. Through the discipline of contemplative prayer, Christian leaders have to learn to listen again and again to the voice of love and to find there the wisdom and courage to address whatever issue presents itself to them. Dealing with burning issues without being rooted in a deep personal relationship with God easily leads to divisiveness because, before we know it, our sense of self is caught up in our opinion about a given subject. But when we are securely rooted in personal intimacy with the source of life, it will be possible to remain flexible without being relativistic, convinced without being rigid, willing to confront without being offensive, gentle and forgiving without being soft, and true witnesses without being manipulative."[7]

◆ In the living of the Christ-life, we are called above all to imitate Jesus in His life of love. Jesus was consistently motivated by love. In the end He was literally consumed by love, for it led Him to a place called Calvary. He was brutally nailed to a cross and raised up midst the laughter and ridicule of enemies. He

*Heart of Jesus, We place our trust in You.*

hung there, bruised and beaten, His body smeared with blood. There was the flush of fever mixed with the chill of approaching death. There was also a great spiritual anguish as He realized that down through the ages many would reject His redemptive love. It was a terrible scene, yet one permeated with a haunting beauty which came forth from the magnificent love of His Heart. His crucified figure, silhouetted against a darkening sky, is the everlasting reminder that to live is to love, and that to love involves not only joy, but also suffering.

◆ St. Bonaventure, doctor of the Church, talks about our union with the Heart of Christ:

"The heart I have found is the heart of my King and Lord, of my Brother and Friend, the most loving Jesus. I say without hesitation that His Heart is also mine. Since Christ is my head, how could that which belongs to my head not also belong to me? As the eyes of my bodily head are truly my own, so also is the heart of my spiritual Head. Oh what a blessed lot is mine to have one Heart with Jesus!"[8]

◆ The following words from John's gospel emphasize the absolute necessity of our union with Jesus:

"I am the true vine, and my Father is the vine dresser. Every branch in me that bears no fruit he cuts away, and every branch that does bear fruit he prunes to make it bear even more. You are pruned already, by means of the word that I have spoken to you. Make your home in me, as I make mine in you. As a branch cannot bear fruit all by itself but must remain part of the vine, neither can you unless you remain in me.

"I am the vine, you are the branches. Whoever remains in me, with me in him, bears fruit in plenty; for cut off from me you can do nothing." (Jn 15: 1-5).

# Thoughts on the Eucharist

The Eucharist is our chief source for growth in the Christ-life. There follow some thoughts on this magnificent Gift of Jesus to us.

◆ When Jesus speaks of His Blood as the "Blood of the Covenant" (Mt 26:28), we are reminded that blood sealed or ratified the Mosaic covenant at Mount Sinai. Moses sprinkled sacrificial blood upon the altar, which represented God, and upon the Jewish people. Because blood was a distinctive symbol of life for the Jewish people, such an action had a deep significance for them. This action of Moses symbolized the sealing or ratification of the covenant—a new life relationship between Yahweh and the Jewish people.

The sacrificial Blood of Jesus has also formed a covenant—the New Covenant. In the shedding of His Blood, Jesus has established a new life relationship between His Father and the human race. Forming a core, focal point of the redeemed human race are the members of the Christian community, the Church. The Eucharist, in recalling and making sacramentally present the shedding of Jesus' covenant Blood, is the Church's great covenant act. The Eucharist sustains the life of the covenant, nourishes it, causes it to grow. Through participation in the Eucharistic liturgy we should be growing in our covenant life. We should be developing a greater love-union with the Father, Son and Holy Spirit. We should be growing in a sense of community, in a deep love for the Church, in a desire to contribute our share to the building up of the body of Christ. We should be learning to curb our selfishness, this selfishness which deadens a dynamic concern for the Christian community and the entire human race. Participation in the Eucharist should also be curbing divisive jealousy, forming us more and more as persons who want deeply to love all so that it can be more often said of us, "See those Christians, how they love one another." The Eucharist can more radically shape us according to these covenant attitudes if we allow it to do so. We repent over the times we have resisted. We rejoice regarding the times we have opened ourselves to the Eucharist's transformative power.

# Mother of Our Christ-life

Mary is the Mother of our Christ-life, this life which flows to us from the bosom of the Father, through Christ, in the Holy Spirit. Pope John Paul II beautifully links Mary's spiritual motherhood toward us with her being Mother of Christ, Mother of the Church, and Model of the Church. "Mary is present in the Church as the Mother of Christ, and at the same time as the Mother whom Christ, in the mystery of the Redemption, gave to humanity in the person of the Apostle John. Thus, in her new motherhood in the Spirit, Mary embraces each and every one in the Church, and embraces each and every one through the Church. In this sense, Mary, Mother of the Church, is also the Church's model. Indeed, as Paul VI hopes and asks: the Church must draw 'from the Virgin Mother of God the most authentic form of perfect imitation of Christ.'"9

# Thoughts on Prayer

Growth in the Christ-life demands a consistent and deepening prayer life. Here are some reflections on prayer:

◆ Fr. John Wright, S.J. tells us: "It is frequently said that the prayer of beginners is more active and that as time goes on and prayer matures it becomes more passive. But it seems to me that we must distinguish here our attitudes and awareness from our actual activities and operations. Initially, our attitude is more active than passive. We are more conscious of doing and acting than of receiving. We are more aware of what we do by way of response than of what God does in His initiative. Gradually this changes, so that we become more and more aware of His action in us, illuminating, inspiring, strengthening, encouraging, and so forth. This means, of course, that our attitude becomes more passive. But our actual activity in operation doesn't itself become less. There is indeed a greater dependence on God's action, and what we do is done more freely, more simply, more intensively and spontaneously. Our attention, then, is more upon God than upon ourselves, but we are actually more active in the real sense. For we see more clearly, believe more deeply, love more purely, rejoice more unselfishly..."[10]

◆ Br. David Steindl-Rast, O.S.B., speaks to us thoughts concerning Vespers, the evening prayer of the Liturgy of the Hours. He talks to us from the setting of his Benedictine monastery: "At Vespers you've put your tools away, taken off your apron, your work clothes, washed up, and put on your robes again. Now you come freshly dressed for the solemn evening celebration at sunset, when darkness descends and the monastery is lit with lamps and candles. It is the hour of peace of heart, of serenity...

"Vespers is the hour that invites peace of heart, which is the reconciling of contradictions within ourselves and round us...

"When evening arrives—no matter what happened during the day, whatever challenges were unmet, whatever disappointments and regrets—people have a universal desire to find a serene place where they can put all the parts of the day together in some tranquil way. Given the spirit of forgiveness of the prior hour, at Vespers we are free to let go of the day and luxuriate in the quiet beauty of the evening.

"The serenity of Vespers, wherein we gather together all the day's contradictions, is truly healing, since healing essentially involves a knitting together of what is apart, what is broken."[11]

# A Sense of Self-Worth

The more we grow in the Christ-life, the more we develop a healthy sense of self-worth. Here are some opportune words regarding this important aspect of our life in Christ: "You need to have a clear idea of your own value and your potential in life. Experts tell us today that many people—especially young people—have such a low opinion of their own worth that they despise, even hate themselves. And so, in a mood of self-hatred, they despair and treat themselves and others in a spirit of revenge.

"But for the person who has accepted Jesus Christ and His teachings, life and self have an eternal value. Each one of us can say, 'Christ shed His precious Blood for me!' Each one of us should think often of the loving kindness of the God who created us, of the generosity of God's Son who suffered to redeem us, of the fact that the Holy Spirit makes our body His temple of grace. We ought to think about the magnificent design of God that is shown in this body and in the creation around us.

"Each one of us should see this life as of eternal importance because it is the introduction to an eternal life with God. We who have the faith know that our challenge is to take this life and make it as much like the Christ-life as possible. This is the Christ-life which St. Ignatius of Antioch called 'our inseparable life!' As the years go on, you are to mature to the fullness of Christ."[12]

# Relationships with Others

Growth in the Christ-life gives us an increased awareness of our relationships with others. That is to say, the true Christian is keenly aware that, to a great degree, God intends each of us to press on toward maturity in the spiritual life through proper relationships with our fellow human beings. Indeed, the Christian imperative reminds us that we are to walk life's path, not in isolation, but hand in hand with our brothers and sisters of the human family.

To authentically relate to others, we must be aware of who they really are. We must be able to penetrate beyond surface appearances, which may or may not be appealing to us, and contact others in their core existence. When we are truly in touch with others at the core of their beings, we are aware of their awesome dignity. We are conscious that these persons are created and redeemed by God in His overwhelming love for them. Fortified with this proper awareness, we are then in a position to relate to others as we should.

In order to be in touch with the inner self of others, we must be aware of or in touch with our own inner or true self. This awareness, in turn, is also an awareness that our self is in the image of God, that we have been divinized in Christ, that we are oriented toward love of God and neighbor. Here, then, we see the profound interaction between the three awarenesses and loves: awareness and love of God, self and neighbor.

As Christians, consequently, we should have a maturing sense of how our existence is, in varied ways, profoundly interlinked with the existence of others. This reality of union with others is not limited to those we directly meet but includes all members of the human family.

# The Christian and the World

God calls us to share His love for His creation. Growth in Christ develops our awareness of this truth. The Christian should have a deeper love for the world than the non-believer. All that is good and true and beautiful, all that we humans reach out for in hope, all the possibilities for our true earthly progress, all the worthwhile and enthusiastic dreams of the human heart for a better world—yes, the Christian should yearn more deeply for all this than the non-believer. Why? Because the Christian knows that the world belongs to Christ. The Christian knows that the human race's pursuit of the true, the good, and the beautiful is ultimately a pursuit of Christ. The Christian knows that any authentic step forward that the human family takes marks a deepening of the Christlike evolutionary process whereby mankind and this world are more fully united to the center and the crown of the universe— Christ Himself.

Obviously, we do not love and embrace the world's sinful dimension. A holy sadness should touch us when we reflect upon the sinful depravity that defiles the world's Christlike image. We do not refuse secular involvement, however, because of the world's sinfulness. We must behave in a way that is different from the way much of the world thinks and acts, yet we must be different in a way that does not make us shirk our responsibility towards the secular. All of us, whether we live within monastery walls or within the explosiveness of the inner city, have this responsibility—each in his or her own way.

# The Priest and the Church

The *Directory on the Ministry and the Life of Priests* tells us:

"Through the mystery of Christ, the priest lives his multiple ministries and is inserted also into the mystery of the Church which 'becomes aware in faith that her being comes not from herself but from the grace of Christ in the Holy Spirit.' In this sense, while the priest is in the church, he is also set in front of it.

"The Sacrament of Holy Orders, in fact, makes the priest a sharer not only in the mystery of Christ, the Priest, Master, Head and Shepherd, but in some way also in Christ, Servant and Spouse of the Church! This is the 'Body' of Him who has loved and loves to the point of giving Himself for her (cf. Eph 5:25); who renews her and purifies her continually by means of the Word of God and of the sacraments (cf. Ibid. 5:26); who works to make her always more beautiful (cf. Ibid., 5:27), and lastly, who nourishes her and treats her with care (cf. Ibid., 5:29).

"The priests, as collaborators of the Episcopal Order, form with their Bishop a sole presbyterate and participate, in a subordinate degree, in the only priesthood of Christ. Similar to the Bishop, they participate in that espousal dimension in relation to the Church which is well expressed in the Rite of the episcopal ordination when the ring is entrusted to them.

"The priest who, 'in the individual local communities of the faithful, makes the Bishop present, so to speak, to whom they are united with a faithful and great spirit,' must be faithful to the Bride and almost like a living icon of Christ, the Spouse, renders fruitful the multiform donation of Christ to His Church.

"By this communion with Christ, the Spouse, the ministerial priesthood is also founded—as Christ, with Christ, and in Christ—in the mystery of transcendent supernatural love of which the marriage among Christians is an image and a participation.

"Called to the act of supernatural love, absolutely gratuitous, the priest should love the Church as Christ has loved her, consecrating to her all his energies and giving himself with pastoral charity in a consummate act of generosity."[13]

# John Paul II on the Priesthood

There follow excerpts from an address given by Pope John-Paul II on October 27, 1995 at a symposium in honor of the 30th anniversary of *Presbyterorum Ordinis*:

◆ **"The priest is a man of the Eucharist.** In the span of nearly 50 years of priesthood, what is still the most important and most sacred moment for me is the celebration of the Eucharist. My awareness of celebrating *in persona* Christ at the altar prevails—*Holy Mass is the absolute center of my life and of every day of my life.* It is at the heart of the theology of priesthood, a theology I learned not so much from text books as from living examples of holy priests. First and foremost, from the holy Curé of Ars, Jean Marie Vianney. Still today I remember his biography written by Fr. Trochu, which literally *overwhelmed me.* I mention the Curé of Ars but he is not the only model of priesthood who impressed me. There were other holy priests whom I admired, having known them either through their biographies or personally, because they were contemporaries. I looked to them and from them I learned what the priesthood is, both as a vocation and as a ministry.

◆ **"The priest is a man of prayer.** 'I nourish you with what I myself live in,' St. Anselm said. The proclaimed truths must be discerned and adopted in the intimacy of prayer and meditation. Our ministry of the word consists in expressing what was first prepared in prayer.

"However, this is not the only dimension of priestly prayer. Since the priest is the mediator between God and man, many turn to him asking for prayers. *This prayer, in a certain sense, 'creates the priest,' especially as Pastor.* And, at the same time, every priest 'creates himself' constantly, through prayer. I am thinking of the marvelous prayer of the Breviary, *Officium Divinum,* in which the whole Church, through the lips of her ministers, prays together with Christ.' I am thinking of the vast numbers of requests and prayer intentions that are constantly presented to me by various people. I take note of the intentions mentioned to us by people from all over the world and I keep them in my chapel on my prie-dieu, so that they are constantly in my mind, even when they cannot literally be repeated every day. There they stay and it can be said that the Lord Jesus knows them for they are among the notes on my prie-dieu and also in my heart.

♦ **"Being priests today.** The theme of priestly identity is always timely because it is a question of our 'being ourselves.' During the Second Vatican Council and immediately afterwards, much was said about this. The problem probably originated in a certain pastoral crisis, in the face of secularization and the abandonment of religious practices. Priests began to wonder: *are we still necessary?* And many priests displayed symptoms of a certain loss of their own identity.

"From the start, as the author of the Letter to the Hebrews wrote, the priest was *'taken from among men and made their representative before God to offer gifts and sacrifices for sins'* (cf. Heb 5: l). This is the best definition of the priest's identity. Every priest, according to the gifts bestowed upon him by the Creator, can serve God in various ways and, with his priestly ministry, can reach various sectors of human life, bringing them closer to God. However, he remains and must remain a man chosen among others and 'made their representative before God.'

"Priestly identity is important for the presbyter; it is important for his *witness among people* who, in him, seek only the priest: *a true 'homo Dei',* who loves the Church as his Bride; who is a *witness to God as the Absolute* and to invisible realities for the faithful; who is a *man of prayer* and, because of this, *a true teacher, guide and friend.* Before a priest like this it is easier for believers to kneel and confess their sins; it is easier for them, when they participate in Mass, to be aware of the anointing of the Holy Spirit, granted to the priests' hands and heart through the sacrament of Holy Orders.

"But how can a priest totally fulfill his vocation? You know the secret well, dear priests: it is by *trusting in God's support and constantly striving for holiness.* This evening I would like to wish each of you 'the grace to rekindle daily the gift of God you have received with the laying on of hands' (cf. Tm 1:6), to feel the comfort of the deep friendship which binds you to Jesus and unites you with one another, the comfort of experiencing the joy of seeing the flock of God grow in an ever greater love for Him and for all people, of cultivating the tranquil conviction that the One who began in you the good work will bring it to completion at the day of Jesus Christ (cf. Phil 1:6).

"May *Mary, most holy, Mary, Mother of priests,* sustain you with her example and her intercession."[14]

# Words from Sri Lanka

One of our priest-readers, Fr. Chryso Pieris, S.J., has written us from far away Sri Lanka:

Dear Fr. Edward,

I began to receive your excellent Newsletter. Thank you.

Here is a small contribution from me, a short note on the Good Shepherd.

God Bless you and your work,
Your brother in Our Lord,
Chryso Pieris, S.J.

And here are his words on the Good Shepherd, some of the most beautiful and inspiring I have ever read:

"I lay down my life for my sheep, said the Good Shepherd. When He did it on the cross, His very detractors proclaimed who the Good Shepherd was. They scoffed: 'He saved others, let Him save Himself.' The first part of the statement is true, they could not deny it, the second part was a challenge they knew in their vile hearts He will not accept. He will save others, but He will never, never save Himself. And the centurion who saw it proclaimed Him the Son of God.

"One could see it all through His life. When a multitude was hungry He gave them to eat, but when He was hungry He would not turn stone to bread. When a wedding party needed wine, He gave them excellent wine, but when He was thirsty on the cross he would not get water or wine from heaven; He got only bitter gall. The young man of Naomi, Lazarus, Jairus' daughter and also the woman caught in adultery; He saved so many lives, but His own He will never, never save. This is the hallmark of the Good Shepherd—utter selflessness. A man so absolutely for others. This is Jesus, the Good Shepherd, the model for all good pastors."

# Act of Consecration

Lord Jesus, Chief Shepherd of the Flock, I consecrate my priestly life to Your Heart, pierced on Calvary for love of us. From Your pierced Heart the Church was born, the Church You have called me, as a priest, to serve in a most special way. You reveal Your Heart as symbol of Your love in all its aspects, including Your most special love for me, whom You have chosen as Your priest-companion. Help me always to pour out my life in love of God and neighbor. Heart of Jesus, I place my trust in You!

Dear Blessed Virgin Mary, I consecrate myself to your maternal and Immaculate Heart, this Heart which is symbol of your life of love. You are the Mother of my Savior. You are also my Mother. You love me with the most special love as this unique priest-son. In a return of love I give myself entirely to your motherly love and protection. You followed Jesus perfectly. You are His first and perfect disciple. Teach me to imitate you in the putting on of Christ. Be my motherly intercessor so that, through your Immaculate Heart, I may be guided to an ever closer union with the pierced Heart of Jesus, Chief Shepherd of the Flock, Who leads me to the Father in the Holy Spirit.

# A Holy Spirit Prayer

The Holy Spirit is given to us to form us more and more according to the image of Christ—to an ever greater growth in the Christ life. Here is a Holy Spirit prayer:

"Come Holy Spirit, Almighty Sanctifier, God of love, who filled the Virgin Mary with grace, who wonderfully changed the hearts of the apostles, who endowed all your martyrs with marvelous courage, come and sanctify us. Enlighten our minds, strengthen our wills, purify our consciences, rectify our judgment, set our hearts on fire, and preserve us from the misfortunes of resisting your inspirations. Amen."

# Letters

We thank all those who have taken the time to write to us. We very much appreciate your letters. Space limitations permit us to publish only a few of these:

Dear Father,
Your publication is most welcome; a breath of fresh air and wisdom.
All the best in Christ,
Don Derivaux
St. Alphonsus Church
McComb, Mississippi

Dear Ed,
Your current Newsletter, December issue, is simply exceptional. Very solid food. I'm reading it very slowly. I especially liked Basil

Pennington's image of the Christlike self.

In Christ Jesus
John Wetmore
Church of St. Stephen, Protomartyr
St. Louis, Missouri

(Dear Father Ed,)
Thank you for the great newsletter. I use it for spiritual reading. It's a great help.

Fr. John Le Voir
Church of the Holy Trinity
South St. Paul, Minnesota

Dear Fr. Ed,
I always enjoy the newsletter. It is always full of such a broad range of solid spiritual and doctrinal authors and topics. Very inspiring! As someone rather newly ordained (Oct., 1993), I'll take all the support and inspiration I can get!

In Christ,
Glenn Eftink
Cathedral of St. Mary of the Annunciation
Cape Girardeau, Missouri

NOTES:

1. Scriptural quotations are taken from *The Jerusalem Bible,* Doubleday & Co.
2. Fr. Joseph Chorpenning, O.S.F.S., as in *The New Dictionary of Catholic Spirituality,* The Liturgical Press, p. 853. (The quotation from St. Francis de Sales is taken from *Treatise on the Love of God,* Tan Books, Vol. 2, p. 280).
3. Msgr. Robert Guste, *The Gift of the Church,* Queenship Publications, pp. 22-23.
4. Fulgentius of Ruspe, as in *The Liturgy of the Hours,* Catholic Book Publishing Co., Vol. III, pp. 97-98.
5. St. John Eudes, as in *The Liturgy of the Hours,* op. cit., Vol. IV, p. 1331.
6. Fr. Lowell Glendon, S.S., as in *The New Dictionary of Catholic Spirituality,* op. cit., pp. 420-421.
7. Fr. Henri Nouwen, *In the Name of Jesus,* Crossroad, pp. 31-32
8. St. Bonaventure, "The Mystical Vine," Ch. 3, "Opera Omnia," Vol. III, as in *Heart of the Redeemer,* Timothy O'Donnell, Trinity Communications, p. 101.
9. Pope John Paul II, *The Mother of the Redeemer,* United States Catholic Conference, No. 38.
10. Fr. John Wright, S.J., *A Theology of Christian Prayer,* Pueblo Pub., p. 101.
11. Br. David Steindl-Rast, O.S.B., *The Music of Silence,* Harper, pp. 101-103.
12. *The Vatican II Sunday Missal,* St. Paul Publications, p. 990.
13. "Directory on the Ministry and Life of Priests," as in special supplement of *Inside the Vatican,* Nos. 12-13.
14. Pope John Paul II, as in *L'Osservatore Romano,* November 15, 1995, English Edition.

A Publication of
Shepherds of Christ
Ministries

# shepherds of Christ

## A SPIRITUALITY NEWSLETTER FOR PRIESTS

MARCH/APRIL 1996

Chief Shepherd of the Flock

# Jesus in His Paschal Mystery

"I am the good shepherd: the good shepherd is one who lays down his life for his sheep. The hired man, since he is not the shepherd and the sheep do not belong to him, abandons the sheep and runs away as soon as he sees a wolf coming, and then the wolf attacks and scatters the sheep. This is because he is only a hired man and has no concern for the sheep. I am the good shepherd. I know my own and my own know me, just as the Father knows me and I know the Father. And I lay down my life for my sheep." (Jn 10:11-15[1]).

He hung upon a cross on a hill called Calvary. Death was near. How much Jesus had already suffered! He had been brutally scourged. Much of His sacred body was a bloody, open wound. He had been derisively crowned with thorns. In a terribly weakened condition, He carried the heavy cross to the hill of Golgotha. There He was stripped of His garments and merci- lessly nailed to the cross. After all this brutal and agonizing suffering, Jesus finally died.

*Have mercy, O Lord, Have mercy on us.*
—The Liturgy of the Hours

Truly the Good Shepherd had laid down His life for His sheep. That mag- nificent Heart, overflowing with love for His Father and all of us, had beat its last.

On the third day, Jesus rose: "Destroy this sanctuary, and in three days I will raise it up! The Jews replied, 'It has taken forty-six years to build this sanctuary: are you going to raise it up in three days?' But he was speaking of the sanctuary that was his body, and when Jesus rose from the dead, his dis- ciples remembered that he had said this, and they believed the scripture and the words he had said." (Jn 2:19-22).

Yes, the Good Shepherd died and rose for our salvation. Behold, the paschal mystery of Jesus!

# Editor's Corner
by Edward Carter S.J.

A number of our entries in this issue of the Newsletter deal explicitly with Christ's paschal mystery, with His death and resurrection. Since we have just recently celebrated the liturgies of Good Friday and Easter, we thought it a particularly apt time to present various ideas concerning the paschal mystery.

Much of the world tries to escape suffering at all possible costs—and many of the escape routes are sinful ones. And such sinful pursuits increase the suffering one is trying to flee.

Certainly we may utilize any means which is according to God's will to alleviate suffering, but to try to escape all suffering is as futile as striving to escape from one's shadow.

As priests we have numerous opportunities to help others properly cope with suffering. The more we ourselves are united with the Christ Who suffered such a brutal death, the more we can help others see God's plan for suffering—that it is meant to lead to greater life. Let us often recall the words of St. Paul:

"For Christ did not send me to baptize, but to preach the Good News, and not to preach that in the terms of philosophy in which the crucifixion of Christ cannot be expressed. The language of the cross may be illogical to those who are not on the way to salvation, but those of us who are on the way see it as God's power to save...And so, while the Jews demand miracles and the Greeks look for wisdom, here we are preaching a crucified Christ; to the Jews an obstacle that they cannot get over, to the pagans madness, but to those who have been called, whether they are Jews or Greeks, a Christ who is the power and the wisdom of God..." (1 Cor 1:17-24).

---

# Thoughts on the Paschal Mystery

The Church in her Good Friday and Easter liturgies has just recently presented to us the paschal mystery of Jesus—His death and resurrection—in a very special way. In saying this we must remember that each Mass of every day makes sacramentally present the death and resurrection of Jesus.

Here are some thoughts concerning Jesus' paschal mystery and our participation in it:

◆ St. Paul tells us: "All I want is to know Christ and the power of his resurrection and to share his sufferings by reproducing the pattern of his death. That is the way I can hope to take my place in the resurrection of the dead." (Phil 3:10-11).

◆ When we are baptized we are incorporated into Christ's paschal mystery of death and resurrection. St. Paul speaks of this marvelous union with Jesus: "You have been taught that when we were baptized in Christ Jesus we were baptized in his death; in other words, when we were baptized we went into the tomb with him and joined him in death, so that as Christ was raised from the dead by the Father's glory, we too might live a new life." (Rom 6:3-4).

Christ has structured the Christian life by the way He lived, died, and rose from the dead. It is obvious, then, as Paul tells us above, that the pattern of death-resurrection must be at the heart of the Church's life. Individually and collectively, we continually die with Christ so that we may continually rise with Him. Thus we pass over in a process of ongoing religious transition to a greater participation in Christ's resurrection. It is true that our participation in Christ's resurrection will reach its completion only in eternity. Nevertheless, we begin the life of resurrection here upon the earth, in the here and now of human life, in the midst of joy and pain; in the experience of success and failure, in the sweat of our brow, in the enjoyment of God's gifts. As Christians, we should have a sense of dynamic growth concerning our here and now life of resurrection.

We cannot maintain the life of resurrection or grow in it without a willingness to suffer. This does not mean that we need to feel overwhelmed and heavily burdened in our lives. The greater portion of suffering for most Christians seems to be an accumulation of ordinary hardships, difficulties, and pains. At times, however, deep suffering, even suffering of agonizing proportions, can enter into one's life. Whether the sufferings one encounters are of either the more ordinary variety or the more rare and extreme type, Christians must convince themselves that to relate properly to the cross is to grow in resurrection, and growth in resurrection means we will also have an increased capacity to help give resurrection to others.

◆ Louis Evely observes: "The blessing of hospitals, of people condemned to death, of sanitariums, of all the places where one suffers, is that there people can be found who know that they need help, who no longer pretend to have no need of God or of anyone, who are freed from this exhausting comedy."[2]

◆ Fr. Edward Leen, C.S.Sp., offers us these insightful words concerning the cross: "The cross, then, can have its degrees. God, by what He directly wills for us, or permits to happen to us, can give it a more intense form, in view of effecting in our souls a deeper purification and, in consequence, a closer contact with Himself. The more thorough the crucifixion that is willingly borne, the greater the degree of happiness, because the more perfectly will God be revealed to the soul."[3]

◆ Fr. Peter van Breeman, S.J., succinctly observes: "We share the death of Christ. We empty ourselves. We enter the tomb, and in this way, we join Christ in his resurrection. We know the power of his resurrection and the peace that it brings with it. We experience the fruitfulness of a new life—new strength envelops us. Our baptism means that we open ourselves to Christ so that his life may continue through us."[4]

◆ Caryll Houselander writes with great sensitivity regarding the second station of the Way of the Cross: "They put His own garments on Him again, and Jesus comes out from the judgment hall of Pilate to receive His cross.

"He comes to it gladly! This is a strange thing, for the cross is a symbol of shame, and it is to be His deathbed. Already He sees the very shape of His death in the wide-spread arms. From this moment He will be inseparable from it, until He dies on it. He will labor and struggle under the weight of it until the end comes. Yet Christ welcomes the cross, He embraces it. He takes it into His arms, as a man takes that which he loves into his arms. He lays His beautiful hands on it tenderly, those strong hands of a carpenter that are so familiar with the touch of wood."[5]

◆ Bill Clarke, S.J., gives a concrete example of how joy and suffering are meant to coexist as he speaks of L'Arche, the community founded by Jean Vanier:

"L'Arche began in France in 1964 to give a permanent home to mentally handicapped adults. It seeks to unite the handicapped and those who assist them in a single community, inspired by a spirit of loving acceptance that will help all its members develop to their fullest potential as human beings...

"Almost everyone who comes to L'Arche is immediately impressed by the spirit of joy that prevails there. Yet anyone who comes to know the community more intimately cannot but be impressed, not to say overwhelmed, by the amount of suffering that is simply a part of its daily life.

"The living out in great intensity of these seemingly opposite experiences of joy and suffering, might be called the particular grace or vocation of L'Arche. Both the suffering and the joy are an integral part of the daily existence, but both have their moments of greater intensity and more external expression. There are the instances of crisis and there is death that crystallizes the suffering. The joy reaches its climax in moments of celebration. The one, however, is never entirely without the other, especially because both find their ultimate meaning in the single mystery—birth, death, and resurrection—the total mystery of life."[6]

◆ To follow Jesus entails a willingness to suffer for Him and His cause. The furthering of any worthwhile cause demands a spirit of sacrifice, a willingness to endure a variety of hardships and difficulties. We cannot expect it to be otherwise regarding the cause of Christ. To follow Jesus, to spread His message, to help further the process of ongoing redemption, all this demands a price.

There is an almost endless variety of pains, sufferings, and difficulties which can arise in following Jesus and promoting His cause. At times seeing few, if any, visible results of our labors, feeling unappreciated, experiencing opposition, sometimes comprehending that we are being hated precisely by some of those whom we are striving to help, at times being laughed at and ridiculed—these are some of the ways we experience the sufferings of an apostle.

The suffering involved in contributing to the process of ongoing redemption is not, however, the complete picture. The happiness resulting from commitment to Christ and His mission far outweighs the hardships. To be aware that one is so intimately loved by Jesus, to experience the satisfaction that one is contributing to a cause that cannot fail, to play a role in helping to bring to others the peace and love of Jesus—all of this makes for a life that has no equal. The committed follower of Christ, experiencing what it means to be closely associated with Jesus, realizes why St. Peter said, "Lord,...it is wonderful for us to be here." (Mt 17:4).

◆ St. Paul strikingly portrays the living of death-resurrection: "We are in difficulties on all sides, but never cornered; we see no answer to our problems, but never despair; we have been persecuted, but never deserted; knocked down, but never killed; always, wherever we may be, we carry with us in our body the death of Jesus, so that the life of Jesus, too, may always be seen in our body. Indeed, while we are still alive, we are consigned to our death every day, for the sake of Jesus, so that in our mortal flesh the life of Jesus, too, may be openly shown." (2 Cor 4:8-11).

◆ St. John of the Cross wrote much about how the cross, properly encountered, always leads to greater life—to a greater share in Christ's resurrection here and hereafter. Here are some of his words regarding this fact:

"Though holy doctors have uncovered many mysteries and wonders, and devout souls have understood them in this earthly condition of ours, yet the greater part still remains to be unfolded by them, and even to be understood by them.

"We must dig deeper in Christ. He is like a rich mine with many pockets

containing treasures: however deep we dig we will never find their end or
their limit. Indeed, in every pocket new seams of fresh riches are discovered
on all sides...

"The gate that gives entry into these riches of His wisdom is the cross;
because it is a narrow gate, while many seek the joys that can be gained
through it, it is given to few to desire to pass through it."[7]

♦ In the Gospel of Luke, Jesus Himself speaks to us about this paschal
mystery, about the necessary connection between the cross and resurrection,
between the cross and life:

"Then he said to them, 'You foolish men! So slow to believe the full message of the prophets! Was it not ordained that the Christ should suffer and so
enter into his glory?' Then, starting with Moses and going through all the
prophets, he explained to them the passages throughout the scriptures that
were about himself." (Lk 24:25-27).

# His Death —

*Antiphon:*
Have mercy, O Lord, have mercy on us!

O Lord Jesus Christ,
At prayer in the Garden of Olives,
Weeping with sadness and fear,
Comforted by an angel.

*Antiphon*

O Lord Jesus Christ,
Betrayed by the kiss of Judas,
Abandoned by your apostles,
Delivered over to sinners.

*Antiphon*

O Lord Jesus Christ,
Buffeted, covered with spittle,
Bruised by the blows of soldiers,
Condemned to die on the cross.

*Antiphon*

O Lord Jesus Christ,
Scourged and crowned with thorns,
Clothed in a robe of purple,
Covered with scorn and shame.

*Antiphon*

O Lord Jesus Christ,
Burdened with your cross,
Mounting even to Calvary,
Bearing the weight of our sins,

   *Antiphon*

O Lord Jesus Christ
Stripped of your garments,
Given gall in your thirst,
Crucified with thieves,

   *Antiphon*

O Lord Jesus Christ
Forgiving your executioners,
Confiding your holy Mother
To your beloved disciple

   *Antiphon*

O Lord Jesus Christ
Breathing forth your spirit
Into the hands of your Father,
Dying for all sinners.[8]

   *Antiphon*

# — and Resurrection!

The day of resurrection!
Earth spread the news abroad;
The Paschal feast of gladness,
The Paschal feast of God.
From death to life eternal,
From earth to heaven's height
Our Saviour Christ has brought us,
The glorious Lord of Light.

Our hearts be free from evil
That we may see aright
The Savior resurrected
In his eternal light;
And hear his message plainly,
Delivered calm and clear:
"Rejoice with me in triumph,
Be glad and do not fear."

Now let the heav'ns be joyful,
And with her song begin,
The whole world keep high triumph
And all that is therein,
Let all things in creation
Their notes of gladness blend,
For Christ the Lord has risen,
Our joy that has no end.[9]

# Thoughts on the Eucharist

The Eucharist is the chief source of growth in the spiritual life. We priests, called to have a special kind of union with Christ, should have a unique desire to grow in appreciation of the Eucharist. It is in the Eucharist that we unite with Jesus' paschal mystery in a special way. Here are some reflections on the Eucharist, Jesus' great gift of love to us:

◆ Pope John Paul II tells us: "The Church and the world have a great need of Eucharistic adoration. Jesus waits for us in the sacrament of love. Let us be generous with our time in going to meet him in adoration and contemplation that is full of faith and ready to make reparation for the great faults and crimes of the world. May our adoration never cease."[10]

◆ Archbishop Luis M. Martinez offers us these inspiring words: "If we could dispose ourselves at least to think about what He suffered for each one of us! Our souls are enveloped in His tenderness and in His pain. We are the fruit of His love and His martyrdom. We increasingly receive His gifts of all kinds. We receive them tranquilly, at times joyfully. But those gifts are marked with the blood of Jesus, the blood from His veins and from his Heart. In order that we might taste the least of His heavenly consolations, Jesus had to taste the gall and vinegar of interior desolation...

"Each communion we receive cost Jesus the sacrifice of Calvary...Holy Communion is a banquet from heaven prepared with the blood of Jesus and the bitterness of His Heart."[11]

# The Priestly Call to Holiness

The priest is called to participate in Jesus' death-resurrection in a most special way. Vatican II speaks to us about the priestly life of holiness. "By the sacrament of orders, priests are configured to Christ the Priest so that as ministers of the Head and co-workers of the episcopal order they can build up and establish His whole Body which is the Church. Already, indeed in the consecration of baptism, like all Christians, they received the sign and the gift of so lofty a vocation and a grace that even despite human weakness they can and must pursue according to the Lord's words: 'You therefore are to be perfect, even as your heavenly Father is perfect.' (Mt 5:48).

"To the acquisition of this perfection, priests are bound by a special claim, since they have been consecrated to God in a new way by the reception of orders. They have become living instruments of Christ the eternal priest so that through the ages they can accomplish His wonderful work of reuniting the whole society of men with heavenly power. Therefore, since every priest in his own way represents Christ Himself, he is enriched with special grace.

"Priestly holiness itself contributes very greatly to a fruitful fulfillment of the priestly ministry. True, the grace of God can complete the work of salvation even through unworthy ministers. Yet ordinarily God desires to manifest His works through those whom we have been made particularly docile to the impulse and guidance of the Holy Spirit. Because of their intimate union with Christ and their holiness of life, these men can say with the apostle: 'It is now no longer I that live, but Christ lives in me' (Gal. 2:20)."[12]

# The Christian and the World

Vatican II reminds us that Christ in His paschal mystery has entered into the world's history, has taken this history to Himself, and has summarized it:

"For God's Word, through whom all things were made, was Himself made flesh and dwelt on the earth of men. Thus He entered the world's history as a perfect man, taking that history up into Himself and summarizing it. He Himself revealed to us that 'God is love' (1 Jn 4:8). At the same time he taught us that the new command of love was the basic law of human perfection and hence of the world's transformation.

"To those, therefore, who believe in divine love, He gives assurance that the way of love lies open to all men and that the effort to establish a universal brotherhood is not a hopeless one. He cautions them at the same time that this love is not something to be reserved for important matters, but must be pursued chiefly in the ordinary circumstances of life.

"Undergoing death itself for all of us sinners, He taught us by example that we too must shoulder that cross which the world and the flesh inflict upon those who search after peace and justice. Appointed Lord by His resurrection and given plenary power in heaven and on earth, Christ is now at work in the hearts of men through the energy of His Spirit. He arouses not only a desire for the age to come, but, by that very fact, he animates, purifies, and strengthens those noble longings too by which the human family strives to make its life more human and to render the whole earth submissive to the goal.

"Now, the gifts of the Spirit are diverse. He calls some to give clear witness to the desire for a heavenly home and to keep that desire green among the human family. He summons others to dedicate themselves to the earthly service of men and to make ready the material of the celestial realm by this ministry of theirs. Yet He frees all of them so that by putting aside love of self and bringing all earthly resources into the service of human life they can devote themselves to that future when humanity itself will become an offering accepted by God.

"The Lord left behind a pledge of this hope and strength for life's journey in that sacrament of faith where natural elements refined by man are changed into His glorified Body and Blood, providing a meal of brotherly solidarity and a foretaste of the heavenly banquet."[13]

# Serving Others

Our participation in Jesus' death-resurrection includes our service of love to others.

In rarer moments of heroic reflection, we perhaps have dreamed of sensational ways through which we may be called to lay down our lives for our neighbor. For most of us, however, such opportunities will probably never occur, and this is just as well. Our courage could well be far less in a real situation than it is in the inflated proportions of dreamlike musings. Most people perform much better in the less heroic atmosphere of everyday sameness. Yet each day, so ordinarily similar to both the one which has preceded and the one which will follow, offers constant opportunities for the laying down of one's life for others. If these daily opportunities are less sensational than the more heroic occasions, they are much more numerous and therefore much more consistently present as possibilities for serving others.

Dying daily for others means many things. It means curbing those persistent, selfish tendencies which, if left unchecked, gradually narrow our vision so that we hardly think of anyone but ourselves. Dying daily for others means working at being kind and patient—seemingly little things, but immensely important in maintaining a spirit of harmony in the course of human affairs. Dying daily for others means fidelity to our work, even though this fidelity must be expressed amid temptations such as discouragement, laziness, and disinterest. Dying daily for our neighbor means these and many other things, some of which we all share in common, some of which are peculiar to each person's uniqueness. One of these common elements is this: dying for others in daily and varied fashion is an expression of our present concern while at the same time it increases our capacity for future love.

Jesus, of course, is our great exemplar regarding the service of others: "You know that among the pagans the rulers lord it over them, and their great men make their authority felt. This is not to happen among you. No; anyone who wants to be great among you must be your servant, and anyone who wants to be first among you must be your slave, just as the Son of Man came not to be served but to serve, and to give his life as a ransom for many." (Mt 20:25-28).

# Pope John Paul II Speaks About Children and All of Us

The children of the world are among our most precious treasures. The Holy Father speaks insightfully about children and all of us:

"Little children very soon learn about life. They watch and imitate the behavior of adults. They rapidly learn love and respect for others, but they also quickly absorb the poison of violence and hatred. Family experiences strongly condition the attitudes which children will assume as adults. Consequently, if the family is the place where children first encounter the world, the family must be for children the first school of peace.

"Parents have an extraordinary opportunity to help their sons and daughters to become aware of this great treasure: the witness of their mutual love. It is by loving each other that they enable the child, from the very first moment of its existence, to grow up in peaceful surroundings, imbued with the positive values which make up the family's true heritage: mutual respect and acceptance, listening, sharing, generosity, forgiveness. Thanks to the sense of working together which these values foster, they provide a true education for peace and make the child, from its earliest years, an active builder of peace.

"Children share with their parents and brothers and sisters the experience of life and hope. They see how life's inevitable trials are met with humility and courage, and they grow up in an atmosphere of esteem for others and respect for opinions different from their own.

"It is above all in the home that, before even a word is spoken, children should experience God's love in the love which surrounds them. In the family they learn that God wants peace and mutual understanding among all human beings, who are called to be one great family.

"Children are not a burden of society; they are not a means of profit or people without rights. Children are precious members of the human family, for they embody its hopes, its expectations and its potential.

"Peace is a gift of God; but man and woman must first accept this gift in order to build a peaceful world. People can do this only if they have a childlike simplicity of heart. This is one of the most profound and paradoxical aspects of the Christian message: to become childlike is more than just a moral requirement but a dimension of the mystery of the Incarnation itself.

"The Son of God did not come in power and glory, as he will at the end of the world, but as a child, needy and poor. Fully sharing our human condition in all things but sin (cf. Heb 4:15), he also took on the frailty and hope for the future which are part of being a child. After that decisive moment for the history of humanity, to despise childhood means to despise the One who showed the greatness of his love by humbling himself and forsaking all glory in order to redeem mankind...

"Jesus asked the disciples to become 'children' again (Mk 10:14-15). Jesus thus turned around our way of thinking. Adults need to learn from children the ways of God: seeing children's capacity for complete trust, adults can learn to cry out with true confidence, 'Abba, Father!'

"To become like a little child—with a complete trust in the Father and with the meekness taught by the Gospel—is not only an ethical imperative: it is a reason for hope. Even where the difficulties are so great as to lead to discouragement and the power of evil so overwhelming as to dishearten,

those who can rediscover the simplicity of a child can begin to hope anew. This is possible above all for those who know they can trust in a God who desires harmony among all persons in the peaceful communion of his kingdom. It is also possible for those who, though not sharing the gift of faith, believe in the values of forgiveness and solidarity and see in them—not without the hidden action of the Spirit—the possibility of renewing the face of the earth.

"It is therefore to men and women of good will that I address this confident appeal. Let us all unite to fight every kind of violence and to conquer war! Let us create the conditions which will ensure that children can receive as the legacy of our generation a more united and fraternal world!"[14]

# Prayer

Our growth according to Jesus' pattern of death-resurrection is impossible without a life of prayer. Growth in prayer not only increases our love of God, but also enhances our loving concern for others.

A great example of this is seen in the study of the prayer life of Catherine of Sienna, saint and doctor of the church. Sr. Mary O'Driscoll, O.P., tells us:

"Twenty-six of Catherine of Siena's prayers have been preserved for us. With one possible exception, they are not prayers that she herself wrote or even dictated to others. Rather, they were transcribed by her followers who were present as she prayed aloud. All of these prayers belong to the last four years of her life. They impress us by their simplicity, their intense concentration on God, who is repeatedly praised and thanked, and their constant desire for the salvation of others...

"As her Prayers make evident, Catherine of Sienna was a great intercessor. In them we find her pleading with God persistently and urgently for mercy for all the world, the Church, the pope, her friends and followers, all in need. It is obvious that she does not regard intercession as merely a passing prayer to God on behalf of one or other persons in time of crisis, but rather as an expression of her deep, loving, permanent commitment both to God and to her neighbors. In Catherine's own life, the importance and intensity of her intercession increased according as her union with God and her concern for others increased. This observation tells us something very significant about the prayer of intercession in the Christian life, namely, that it is not, as is sometimes thought, a type of prayer which one passes on the way to the heights of mystical prayer, as though intercession were for beginners and mysticism for those who are advanced in the spiritual life, but as a type of prayer which belongs most particularly to the life of contemplative union with God."[15]

# Act of Consecration

Lord Jesus, Chief Shepherd of the Flock, I consecrate my priestly life to your Heart, pierced on Calvary for love of us. From your pierced Heart the Church was born, the Church you have called me, as a priest, to serve in a most special way. You reveal Your Heart as symbol of Your love in all its aspects, including Your most special love for me, whom you have chosen as Your priest-companion. Help me always to pour out my life in love of God and neighbor. Heart of Jesus, I place my trust in you!

Dear Blessed Virgin Mary, I consecrate myself to your maternal and Immaculate Heart, this Heart which is symbol of your life of love. You are the Mother of my Savior. You are also my Mother. You love me with the most special love as this unique priest-son. In a return of love I give myself entirely to your motherly love and protection. You followed Jesus perfectly. You are His first and perfect disciple. Teach me to imitate you in the putting on of Christ. Be my motherly intercessor so that, through your Immaculate Heart, I may be guided to an ever closer union with the pierced heart of Jesus, Chief Shepherd of the Flock, who leads me to the Father in the Holy Spirit.

# The Holy Spirit in Our Lives

The Holy Spirit desires to fashion us into an ever greater likeness of Christ according to Jesus' pattern of death-resurrection. Mary our Mother cooperates with the Spirit, whose spouse she is, in this process. Obviously, we should pray to the Holy Spirit each day. There are many ways we can do this. We can do this by simply turning our attention to the Spirit at various times during the day as we ask for His guidance. This method can also be complemented by saying certain established prayers. Here is a Holy Spirit prayer from the Church's Liturgy of the Hours:

Father, Lord of earth and heaven,
  King to whom all gifts belong,
Give Your greatest Gift, your Spirit,
  God the holy, God the strong.

Son of God, enthroned in glory,
  Send your promised Gift of grace,
Make Your Church Your holy Temple,
  God the Spirit's dwelling place.

Spirit, come, in peace descending
  As at Jordan, heav'nly Dove,
Seal Your Church as God's anointed,
  Set our hearts on fire with love.

Stay among us, God the Father,
  Stay among us, God the Son,
Stay among us, Holy Spirit:
  Dwell within us, make us one.[16]

# Letters

We thank all those who have taken the time to write to us. We very much appreciate your letters. Space limitations permit us to publish only a few of these:

Dear Fr. Carter,
  Thank you for your valuable newsletter of spirituality for priests.

Fraternally,
Msgr. Walter Schroeder
Church of the Magdalene
North Tarrytown, New York

Dear Ed,

I've read every issue of *Shepherds of Christ,* which is rather rare, because I've received a ton of junk mail every day. Thanks for taking time out to share your inspiring reflections with us who are "too busy."

Just a token to defray some of your costs.

In Christ,
Msgr. Dominic M. Luong
Mary Queen of Vietnam Church
New Orleans, Louisiana


Dear Father Ed,

Thank you for your Nov/Dec Newsletter. Some paragraphs are clearly gifts of the Holy Spirit for me. Keep up the great work for Jesus Christ.

In JMJ,
Gus Biehl, S.M.
East St. Louis, Illinois

Dear Fr. Carter,

Thank you for your most welcome newsletter. I read it gradually, one section at a time, so I can sit with and let sink in the penetrating thoughts you have gleaned from a wonderful variety of sources. If it weren't for this well-chosen digest I would not meet some of the spiritual writers you feature. Yours is an excellent resource for contemplatives on a tight schedule.

In Christ's peace,
Frank Desiderio, C.S.P.
St. Paul's College
Washington, D.C.


Greetings!

I am enclosing a donation for Shepherds of Christ which I find uplifting and inspiring.

Rev. Gino Dalpiaz, C.S.
Scalabrini Mission Center
Stone Park, Illinois


NOTES:
1. Scriptural quotations are taken from *The Jerusalem Bible,* Doubleday & Co.
2. Luis Evely, *Suffering,* Herder & Herder, p. 96.
3. Fr. Edward Leen, C.S.Sp., *Why the Cross?,* Sheed and Ward,
   pp. 95-96.
4. Fr. Peter van Breeman, S.J., *As Bread That is Broken,*
   Dimension, p. 95.
5. Caryll Houselander, *The Way of the Cross,* Sheed and Ward,
   p. 21.
6. Bill Clarke, S.J., *Enough Room for Joy,* Paulist Press,
   pp 13 and 71.

7. St. John of the Cross, as in *The Liturgy of the Hours,* Catholic Book Publishing Co., Vol I, pp. 1246-1247.
8. *The Liturgy of the Hours,* op. cit., Vol II, p. 403.
9. Ibid., p. 543.
10. Pope John Paul II, "On the Mystery of and Worship of the Holy Eucharist", April 1980, as in *Apostles of the Holy Spirit Bulletin,* Winter 1995.
11. Archbishop Luis Martinez, *Only Jesus,* B. Herder Book Co., pp. 212-213.
12. *The Documents of Vatican II,* "Decree on the Ministry and Life of Priests," America Press Edition, Ch 3, No. 12.
13. Ibid., "Pastoral Constitution on the Church in the Modern World," No. 38.
14. Pope John Paul II, "Let us Give Children a Future of Peace," Dec. 8, 1995, as in *Inside the Vatican,* February, 1996.
15. *Catherine of Siena, Selected Writings,* ed., Mary O'Driscoll, O.P., New City Press, p. 50.
16. *The Liturgy of the Hours,* op. cit., Vol. II, p. 1027.

A Publication of
Shepherds of Christ
Ministries

# shepherds of Christ

## A SPIRITUALITY NEWSLETTER FOR PRIESTS

MAY/JUNE 1996

Chief Shepherd of the Flock

# Christ and His Church

"I am the good shepherd: the good shepherd is one who lays down his life for his sheep. The hired man, since he is not the shepherd and the sheep do not belong to him, abandons the sheep and runs away as soon as he sees a wolf coming, and then the wolf attacks and scatters the sheep. This is because he is only a hired man and has no concern for the sheep. I am the good shepherd. I know my own and my own know me, just as the Father knows me and I know the Father. And I lay down my life for my sheep." (Jn 10:11-15[1])

Yes, the Good Shepherd has laid down His life for His sheep. The Good Shepherd's magnificent Heart, overflowing with love for the Father and all of us, was pierced so that the waters of our salvation might flow forth: "It was Preparation Day, and to prevent the bodies remaining on the cross during the sabbath—since that sabbath was a day of special solemnity—the Jews asked Pilate to have the legs broken and the bodies taken away. Consequently the soldiers came and broke the legs of the first man who had been crucified with him and then of the other. When they came to Jesus, they found he was already dead, and so instead of breaking his legs one of the soldiers pierced his side with a lance; and immediately there came out blood and water." (Jn 19:31-34).

Bonaventure, the Franciscan saint and doctor of the Church, comments on the pierced Heart of the Good Shepherd: "Then, in order that the Church might be formed out of the side of Christ sleeping on the cross…the divine plan permitted that one of the soldiers pierce open His sacred side with a lance. While blood mixed with water flowed, the price of our salvation was poured forth, which gushing forth from the sacred fountain of the heart, gave power to the sacraments of the Church…"[2]

And very importantly, the Second Vatican itself tells us: "The wonders wrought by God among the people of the Old Testament were but a prelude to the work of Christ the lord in redeeming mankind and giving perfect glory to God. He achieved His task principally by the paschal mystery of His blessed passion, resurrection from the dead, and glorious ascension, whereby 'dying, he destroyed our death, and, rising, he restored our life.' For it

# Editor's Corner

by Edward Carter S.J.

One of the main themes of this issue of the newsletter is that of Church. In our editor's column, we wish to add a few more ideas about the Church.

We must all strive to grow in a sense of corporateness. We have to always strive to stretch our vision and be aware that we are members of the universal Church, as, at the same time, we are members of a particular parish and diocese. We must think in terms of what is good for the entire Church, and through the Church of what is good for the entire human race. We must be selfless, working for the good of the whole. Even when we disagree, we do so not that we may appear to have the upper hand, but because we believe that to disagree here and now is necessary so that the truth may better emerge. St. Paul speaks to us about the sense of corporateness:

"If our life in Christ means anything to you, if love can persuade at all, or the Spirit that we have in common, or any tenderness and sympathy, then be united in your convictions and united in your love, with a common purpose and a common mind. That is the one thing which would make me completely happy. There must be no competition among you, no conceit, but everybody is to be self-effacing. Always consider the other person to be better than yourself, so that nobody thinks of his own interests first but everybody thinks of other people's interests instead. In your minds you must be the same as Christ Jesus." (Phil 2:1-5)

---

*Christ and His Church* continued from page 139

was from the side of Christ, as He slept the sleep of death upon the cross that there came forth the wonderful sacrament which is the whole Church."[3]

Yes, the Church was born from the pierced side of the Good Shepherd. The Church today is existing in very critical times. The world is experiencing a great multitude of problems, some of these most critical ones. The Church herself, which is a God-given source of light to the world, is herself beset with numerous challenges and problems. One of these problems is the numerous types of divisions existent in the Church. These are hampering her ability to be a light to this troubled world.

We priests, through the sacrament of orders, have been brought into a very special union with Christ. The interests of Christ must, consequently, be the interests of the priest in a most special manner. Consequently, since Christ has a most passionate love for His Church, the priest must strive to imitate this love. The priest must have a deep desire to help heal the wounds of the Church. He must have a burning desire to help her be more what God destines her to be. We must help her become a brighter light to lead a troubled world back to God.

# Thoughts on the Church Today

◆ "Now you together are Christ's body; but each of you is a different part of it. In the Church, God has given the first place to apostles, the second to prophets, the third to teachers; after them, miracles, and after them the gift of healing; helpers, good leaders, those with many languages. Are all of them apostles, or all of them prophets, or all of them teachers? Do they all have this gift of miracles, or all have the gift of healing? Do all speak strange languages, and all interpret them?" (1 Cor 12:27-30)

◆ The Church as Body of Christ is the earthly, visible continuation of the Incarnation. Christ is the Head of the Body, we are His members. Since the Church is the terrestrial manifestation of the mystery of Christ, her life is patterned after His. The various mysteries or events of Christ, especially the central ones of death and resurrection, are to be relived by the Church's members. Indeed, the image of the Church is a Christlike one.

For the Church to be constituted in the image of Christ is both a great privilege and a great responsibility. The more the Church can project the image of Christ, the more she is capable of being an instrument of continued redemption. Jesus led a life of material simplicity. Is this characteristic sufficiently manifest in the life of the Church? Jesus came to minister, not to be served. Do we as members of the Church properly project to one another and to the world an attitude of loving service? Jesus manifested a special concern for the poor, the lowly, the helpless. Do we do likewise? Jesus hungered and thirsted for justice's sake. Do the many flagrant violations of justice in our own day really bother us? Jesus loved each individual and forgave His enemies. Do we love everybody and do we forgive? Jesus was ridiculed, rejected, spat upon, beaten, crowned with thorns, abandoned by His friends, lifted up on a cross. This was all a proof of how much He loved His Church and the world. How much are we willing to suffer for the Church and the world?

◆ Vatican II speaks concerning the Church and its relationship with the world: "Though mankind today is struck with wonder at its own discoveries and its power, it often raises anxious questions about the current trend of the world, about the place and role of man in the universe, about the meaning of the universe, about the meaning of his individual and collective strivings, and about the ultimate destiny of reality and of humanity. Hence, giving witness and voice to the faith of the whole People of God gathered together by Christ, this Council can provide no more eloquent proof of its solidarity with the entire human family with which it is bound up, as well as its respect and love for that family, than by engaging with it in conversation about the various problems.

"The Council brings to mankind light kindled from the gospel, and puts at its disposal those saving resources which the Church herself, under the guidance of the Holy Spirit, receives from her Founder. For the human person deserves to be preserved; human society deserves to be renewed. Hence the pivotal point of our total presentation will be man himself, whole and entire, body and soul, heart and conscience, mind and will.

"Therefore this sacred Synod proclaims the highest destiny of man and champions the godlike seed which has been sown in him. It offers to mankind the honest assistance of the Church in fostering that brotherhood of all men which corresponds to this destiny of theirs. Inspired by no earthly ambition, the Church seeks but a solitary goal: to carry forward the work of Christ Himself under the lead of the befriending Spirit. And Christ entered this world to give witness to the truth, to rescue and not to sit in judgment, to serve and not be served."[4]

♦ There is an errant philosophy of individualism rampant in today's world that can certainly influence the contemporary Christian. This philosophy is patently false. It provides a type of individualism that is inimical to community because it teaches that one must look out for oneself regardless of the consequences to others. Do your own thing, in other words, whenever and wherever you please, and let the chips fall where they may. This type of individualism is obviously wrong and pernicious.

There is, on the other hand, a kind of individualism that is positive and in perfect harmony with the tenets of community, and, in our present context, with life within the Church: "An absolutely individual Christianity in the most personal experience of grace and ecclesial Christianity are no more radically opposed than are body and soul, than are man's transcendental essence and his historical constitution, or than are individuality and intercommunication. The two condition each other mutually. The very thing which we are from God is mediated in the concreteness of history by what we call church. And it is only in and through this mediation that it becomes our own reality and our salvation in full measure. For this reason church exists and has to exist."[5]

♦ The above remarks easily lead us to a quotation of John Henry Cardinal Newman. Newman's words remind us that each of us has a God-given role to fulfill in the Church, and that no one else can accomplish this mission. This is a great privilege, and a great responsibility: "Everyone who breathes, high and low, educated and ignorant, young and old, man and woman, has a mission, has a work. We are not sent into this world for nothing, we are not born at random...God sees every one of us. He creates every soul, He lodges it in a body, one by one, for a purpose."[6]

◆ Here are words of Pope John Paul II to a group of seminarians: "As you know, I have just had a long working session with your bishops. It was a particularly important conversation, in the course of which we were able, we who are jointly in charge of all the churches, to face up to our responsibilities in order to assume them according to what pleases God. And now, it

seems quite natural to continue this conversation, in a way, with those who are preparing to become collaborators of the episcopal order, and to be associated in this way, in the Person of Christ, with the preaching of the Gospel and the guidance of the People of God. You are still young, certainly, but already you divine a great many things. You understand that your gift must be complete and that, the further you go, the more you will discover the necessity of making it—if I may venture to say so—even more complete. It is at this level, therefore, that I will take up my position with you, taking into account, of course, the

fact that a way such as yours takes time, and a long spiritual, intellectual and pastoral maturation, and that the mere desire to become a priest is not enough in itself to meet the requirements of the priesthood.

"One of these requirements, the most fundamental one, is that you should be deeply rooted in Jesus Christ. I invite you to this with all my heart. If you could learn, through prayer and contemplation, to live, preach, love and suffer like Christ, it seems that the main lines of your mission would gradually take shape clearly, and that you would also feel a vital need to join men and bring them what they really need. In such a proceeding, there is already the soul of the apostolate, so that 'action' is indissolubly linked with 'being', and vice versa. Here it is not useful to pursue vain discussions, nor is it good to prefer one to the detriment of the other. The Church intends to form you in complete interior unity, in which the mission requires intimacy with God, and in which the latter calls for the former.

"Do you want to be yourselves, 'good shepherds'? The good shepherd gives his life, and he gives his life for his sheep. Very well, then! It is necessary to discover the sense of self-sacrifice, linked with the sacrifice of Christ, and offer yourselves for others, who expect this witness from you. That can be said of all the faithful, but with all the more reason and in a very special way of priests and future priests. May your daily participation in the Eucharist, and the efforts you make to increase Eucharistic devotion within you, keep you along this way!"[7]

◆ The People of God are just that, people, and this implies that they are subject to imperfections and sinfulness like the rest of the human race. The Church is a pilgrim Church, made up of people struggling to be good, but at times failing, sinning, neglecting to live the Gospel ideal as well as they ought. But a pilgrim Church must endure this darker side of human nature. The pilgrim Church is still on its way, having much of the journey yet to travel. The pilgrim Church is in need of constant conversion of heart as it keeps reaching out to assimilate the Gospel of Jesus in deeper faith, hope and love.

Despite the imperfections and sinfulness of the Church, we should always be striving to love more loyally this organization which is the Body of Christ. We are to love the Church, not with a blind loyalty which covers over her faults and blemishes and sinfulness, but with a loyalty that strives to help the Church become more what she should be. We are also to love the Church in a way which allows us not only to look at what is wrong with her, but which also permits us to see all that is right with her. We are to love the Church as a gift coming forth from the pierced Heart of Jesus. To fail to love this  Church, then, is to fail to love this precious gift which Jesus has left us in the shedding of His blood. Christ and His Church are inseparably connected. To grow in love of Christ is to grow in love of His Church.

◆ In so many different ways we receive support from this organization called Church. Certain disillusioned members of the Church think they could better go it alone in trying to live the Gospel and in trying to influence social structures with Christian principles. They forget how much support they have received from the institutional Church. Donald Thorman, when he was editor of *The National Catholic Reporter* (a publication which has not hesitated to point out the faults of the institutional Church) observed: "Of course, there are many...cases in which the individual carries the burden of witnessing for Christ and the Christian message through his presence in the civic and social community. But without the 'support system' of an organized Church, which preached to him, helped prepare and motivate him, and which now continues to support him liturgically and educationally, his chances of maintaining himself without such support are negligible."[8]

◆ Vatican II clearly reminds us that the Church's life is centered in her liturgy: "...the liturgy is the summit toward which the activity of the church is directed; at the same time it is the fountain from which all her power flows. For the goal of apostolic works is that all who are made sons of God by faith and baptism should come together to praise God in the midst of His Church, to take part in her sacrifice, and to eat the Lord's supper.

"The liturgy in its turn inspires the faithful to become 'of one heart in love' when they have tasted to their full of the paschal mysteries; it prays that 'they may grasp by deed what they hold by creed.' The renewal in the Eucharist of the covenant between the Lord and man draws the faithful into the compelling love of Christ and sets them afire. From the liturgy, therefore, and especially from the Eucharist, as from a fountain, grace is channeled into us; and the sanctification of men in Christ and the glorification of God, to which all the other activities of the Church are directed as toward their goal, are most powerfully achieved."[9]

# The Father: Origin of the Church's Life

Archbishop Joseph Raya of the Byzantine Rite states: "The Father is the source of all life and love. In our liturgical life no action of Christ or of the Holy Spirit is ever mentioned without mentioning the Father as its source and origin. He is the principle and essence of being and movement. he is the very source of everything, first of all within the Trinity itself, and then in all of creation."[10]

The life of the Church flows from the bosom of the Father through the Son and in the Holy Spirit. Mary, as Mother of the Church, intercedes regarding all aspects of the Church's life.

# The Spirit Is Present

We have just celebrated the great Feast of Pentecost. It is appropriate, then, for us to reflect upon this great Gift to the Church, the Holy Spirit.

The Spirit is present. He is present in our midst—present to the world, to the Church, to each of us individually. He is among us to deepen the Christlike design upon the world, that Christlike image which Christ has imprinted through His life, death and resurrection. The Spirit is present to make us more alive, to stir up deep desires which make us thirst for God, desires which also make us more aware of what it means to love our neighbor. In the fourth Eucharistic prayer we say:

"Father, you so loved the world that in the fullness of time you sent your only Son to be our Savior...In fulfillment of your will he gave himself up to death, but by rising from the dead, he destroyed death and restored life. And that we might live no longer for ourselves but for him, he sent the Holy Spirit from you, Father, as his first gift to those who believe, to complete his work on earth and bring us the fullness of grace".[11]

God is a God of life. The Spirit is present to us in order that we may have life and have it more abundantly. The Spirit does not in any way destroy or lessen anything which is authentically human. His grace rather elevates human nature to a new life, perfects it, gives it a new dynamism.

At times we tend to shy away from the action of the Spirit, erroneously thinking that if we abandon ourselves to His touch, life will be less than we want it to be, different than we want it to be. We mistakenly think that a life in the Spirit will somehow diminish our zest for living, that it will lessen our capacity for human happiness and fulfillment. If we succumb to such thinking, our self-made images of what happiness is, or what contributes to it, become mirages. These mirages delude us, as the mirages on the horizon delude the desert traveler. They never give us the happiness they seem to promise.

The truth is that life in the Spirit, the Christ-life, gives us an increased capacity to be alive, vital, happy. Our life in Christ, under the Spirit's touch, permeates our total existence, infuses our being with a newness, which, if we give ourselves to it, brings a happiness and fullness of life impossible to the person who refuses the Spirit's gift.

The Christian life is human life in the spirit—divinized human life. Life in the Spirit is a man deeply and tenderly loving his wife, a friend sharing with friend. Life in the Spirit is our work life. It is being a nurse, a mother and wife, a pastor, a teacher, a laborer, a scientist, a business man. Life in the Spirit is a person at play. Life in the Spirit is laughing, rejoicing, being thrilled by nature's beauty, being eager for life's possibilities. Life in the Spirit is believing, trusting loving. It is also weeping, being crushed by sorrow, losing a loved one, experiencing failure.

The above described human experiences, and all others, too, comprise life in the Spirit as long as they come under His guidance. If these experiences are regulated by the divine will, they are expressions of our Christ-life. This is the biblical sense of life in the Spirit. It is the redeemed person living as he or she should. It does not matter what the action or experience happens to be at the moment, as long as the touch of the Spirit is present.

The spiritual person, then, is the one who is careful to submit one's life to the guidance of the Spirit.

The unspiritual person, on the other hand, is one who lives not according to the Spirit, but according to the flesh. This biblical concept of living according to the flesh refers to sins of one's total person, both spirit and body, not only those involving the flesh. Living according to the flesh includes everything which is not directed by the Spirit. If it includes sexual sins and other failings of the flesh, it also embraces all failings of the spirit. Life according to the flesh is intellectual pride. It is working at one's profession for selfish motives. It is jealousy, sloth, and unjust anger. It is thinking too much about oneself. It is a lack of concern for the human dignity of the other. Life in the flesh is cheating in business; it is a greed for power; it is racial hatred; it is a callous unconcern about social injustice. Life in the flesh, then, is life outside God's redemptive plan. It is those actions and attitudes which are against God's will. It is life which refuses to be Spirit-guided.

Life lived according to the Spirit rather than according to the flesh obviously is not always easy. The opposition between the two forces within us is brought out by St. Paul: "When selfish indulgence is at work the results are obvious: fornication, gross indecency and sexual irresponsibility; idolatry and sorcery; feuds and wrangling; jealousy, bad temper and quarrels; disagreements, factions, envy; drunkenness, orgies and similar things. I warn you now, as I warned you before: those who behave like this will not inherit the kingdom of God. What the Spirit brings is very different: love, joy, peace, patience, kindness, goodness, trustfulness, gentleness and self-control...You cannot belong to Christ Jesus unless you crucify all self-indulgent passions and desires.

"Since the Spirit is our life, let us be directed by the Spirit. We must stop being conceited, provocative and envious." (Gal 5:19-26)

The new life which God gives us in the Spirit is patterned after the teaching and example of Jesus. The task of the Spirit is to lead us along the way of Jesus to the Father. His task is to deepen the image of Christ upon us. Because the Spirit knows we cannot closely follow Christ unless we deeply love Him, the Spirit is always inspiring us to a closer love-union with Jesus. We can resist the Spirit's inspiration, as we too well know, and when we do, we are tarnishing the name "Christian" which we profess. The word "Christian" should ideally mean a person completely dedicated to Jesus Christ, one on fire with love of Him, one eager to promote His cause. The committed Christian, in his or her own way, has to imitate the Christlike enthusiasm of St. Paul: "Life to me, of course, is Christ, but then death would bring me something more; but then again, if living in this body means doing work which is having good results—I do not know what I should choose. I am caught in this dilemma: I want to be gone and be with Christ, which would be very much the better, but for me to stay alive in this body is a more urgent need for your sake." (Phil 1:21-24)

The Spirit is present. He is with us to fashion us more and more according to the image of Christ as He deepens our incorporation into the life, death and resurrection of Christ. And as the Spirit first gave us Christ through Mary, He continues to use Mary's cooperation as He causes our growth in Christ. As we open ourselves to the touch of the Spirit, we are fulfilling the Father's plan for us: "We knew that by turning everything to their good God cooperates with all those who love him, with all those that he has called according to his purpose. They are the ones he chose specially long ago and intended to become true images of his Son...." (Rom 8: 28-29).

# The Heart of Christ

We have just reflected on how the Holy Spirit labors within us to deepen our love for Christ, how He wishes to give us a burning desire to give our all for our magnificent Savior, this Jesus Who died a brutal and agonizing death for you and for me, this Jesus from Whose pierced Heart the Church was born.

Oh, how glorious would be the Church's existence if many more of her members would be on fire with love for Christ! They would have a burning and all-consuming desire to help spread Christ's magnificent love in ever greater measure to the whole world.

Our task as priests is to help lead the members of the Church to this kind of deep love for Jesus Christ. Obviously, the deeper our own love for Jesus, the more able we are to help others grow in an enthusiastic love for Him, a love which helps to renew the Church and the world.

One of the great ways God has given us to aid us in developing a deep love relationship with Jesus is devotion to the Heart of Christ. In the preface of the Mass for the Feast of the Sacred Heart, a Feast which we have recently celebrated, the Church invites all her members to come to the pierced Heart of Jesus for life-giving graces:

"Lifted high on the cross,
Christ gave his life for us,
so much did he love us.
From his wounded side flowed blood and water,
the fountain of sacramental life in the Church.
To his open heart the Savior invites all men,
to draw water in joy from the springs of salvation."[12]

St. Peter Canisius, doctor of the Church, is an outstanding example of one who drank deeply from the Heart of Christ. In doing so, this man of brilliant intellect, became a great saint. In the office for his feast, April 27, we are told:

"St. Peter Canisius is rightly known as the second apostle of Germany. On receiving the apostolic blessing before setting out for that country, he was favored with a mystical experience which he described as follows: 'Eternal High Priest, in your great goodness it pleases you that I should seek from your Apostles confirmation and success for the apostolic blessing I had received.

"'For pilgrims come to pray to them in the Vatican, and there, by your power, they work miracles. I experienced there a great consolation and the same sense of the presence of your grace which was being offered to me through their intercession. They gave me their blessing too, confirmed my mission to Germany and seemed to be promising me their goodwill as apostle of

*Heart of Jesus, We place our trust in You.*

Germany. You know, Lord, how urgently and how often that day you entrusted Germany to me, telling me ever after to have her good at heart, and to wish to live and die on her behalf.

"'Finally, my Saviour, I seemed to be gazing at the Heart of your Sacred Body with my own eyes. It was as if you opened to me and told me to drink from it as from a spring, inviting me to draw the waters of salvation from these springs of yours. I was filled with longing that the waters of faith, hope and charity should flow from your Heart into me. I thirsted for poverty, chastity and obedience; I begged you to wash me all over and dress me in fine clothing. Then I dared to touch your beloved Heart and bury my thirst in it; and you promised me a robe woven in three parts to cover my naked soul and help me greatly in my undertaking. Those three parts were peace, love and perseverance. Secure in the protection of this garment, I was confident that I would lack nothing, and that everything would turn out for your glory.'"[13]

# This Friend Jesus

"I shall not call you servants any more, because a servant does not know his master's business; I call you friends, because I have made known to you everything I have learned from my Father." (Jn 15:15)

What graciousness on the part of Jesus! Our God, our Savior, invites us to be His friends! Indeed, he calls us to the closest friendship with Himself. Here are some thoughts on friendship with Jesus:

"Friendship is a process of self-liberation. As I give myself to another in friendship, I am aided in the process of escape from my false self. I am aided in the process of achieving true self-identity. The facade of the false self more and more recedes through the dynamics of friendship. Why is this? When another receives me in friendship that other receives me as I am. The friend loves me in my good points, loves me despite my bad points. In the warmth of this receptive love, I am encouraged to be and to become my authentic self. I do not have to project a false self, since I know the other will not reject me. Actually, my true self is more attractive to the friend and to others precisely because it is my authentic self—the self God destines me to be, possessing the personal uniqueness with which He has permeated my being.

"Friendships, therefore, increase my freedom—the freedom to be my real self. The deeper an authentic friendship, the more I am encouraged by the other's love to be and to become. I am encouraged to exercise my talents and to develop them to ever greater heights in the loving service of God and others.

"If friendship with a human person increases my growth potential, what are we to say about friendship with Jesus? There is no comparison. Jesus offers me such magnificent opportunities for growth. The more I am aware of Jesus' tremendous and personal love for me, the more secure I feel in developing my real self.

"Being accepted by Jesus as a friend should radically change my life. As Jesus has given Himself entirely to me, so I should give myself entirely to Him. This deep and intense friendship accomplishes my ongoing transformation. This friend, Jesus, through the strength and tenderness of His love, gradually and increasingly draws me out of my selfish traits. He gradually makes me more free to really be. He increasingly assists me in allowing my Christlike-Trinitarian self to emerge more and more in expressions of love for God and neighbor.

"As I share the pleasant experiences of life with this friend, Jesus, He enhances my joy. Being loved and accepted by others, enjoying the challenges and success of work, experiencing simple joys as well as moments of overwhelming happiness, drinking in the breathless beauties of nature— these and all such experiences take on deeper meaning in the presence of Jesus.

"As I share the difficult aspects of human life with Jesus, He lessens their burden. If Jesus is my friend, should I ever capitulate to discouragement? If Jesus is my friend, should a sense of failure ever extinguish my determination to struggle on? If Jesus is my friend, can I ever allow suffering to make me bitter?

"As I strive to grow into a mature Christian, this friend Jesus is profoundly present to me. He is strong, tender, understanding, gentle, loving. He sympathizes, encourages, challenges, inspires. He leads, but does not force. He admonishes us when we are wrong, but He does not reject us. He is overjoyed at our good deeds, yet gently but firmly reminds us that there is still much to accomplish as He guides us in the Spirit to the Father. Jesus is the perfect friend. He is your friend and my friend."[14]

# An Appeal for the Church in Ukraine

Recently I had the great privilege of visiting Slovakia and Ukraine and of witnessing how the Church in these countries is courageously struggling to rebuild itself after years of communist domination. The Church in these areas suffered greatly under communism, and now suffers in a different way as her people face enormous problems in establishing a post-communism existence. These people desperately need our prayers and material assistance.

I made my visit in connection with a wonderful group of people from St. Thomas More parish in Englewood, Colorado. A few years ago this parish, under the leadership of the pastor, Fr. Mike Walsh, instituted a mission organization called Queen of the Apostles Missionary Association—QAMA—to help the struggling Church in the former Soviet Union countries. This organization has truly accomplished marvels within a very short period. Within this issue of the newsletter there is an insert describing QAMA and its activities. Here is the opening paragraph of the insert: "Answering the Gospel command to teach the good news, the call of Vatican II that the laity do their part in evangelizing, mindful of the Holy Father's exhortation on evangelization for the third millennium, recalling the Fatima messages for the conversion of Russia and influenced by past and present-day mystics, a group of Catholic lay men and women met a few years ago to pray at St. Thomas More Church in Englewood, Colorado, and decided to answer the call. Their special challenge would be helping the struggling Church in the former Soviet Union countries." I urge you to take the time to read the entire insert. — *Editor*

# Prayer

Pope Paul VI has left us these words concerning the rosary: "As a Gospel prayer, centered in the mystery of the redemptive Incarnation, the Rosary is therefore a prayer with a clearly Christological orientation...The Jesus that each Hail Mary recalls is the same Jesus Whom the succession of the mysteries proposes to us." And then the Pope emphasizes the need of contemplation as we pray the rosary: "Without this (the Rosary) is a body without a soul, and the recitation is in danger of becoming a mechanical repetition of formulas...By its nature the recitation of the Rosary calls for a quiet rhythm and a lingering pace, helping the individual to meditate on the mysteries of the Lord's life as seen through the eyes of her who was closest to the Lord. In this way the unfathomable riches of these mysteries are unfolded."[15]

# Rosary Reflections

Here are some reflections on the Glorious Mystery of The Resurrection:
"See vividly before your eyes the body of Jesus as He hung on the cross, covered with blood and withered. Picture this in your mind so clear, see His body so battered and so bruised, and next to this picture see the Almighty God as He rose victorious on the third day. See Him adorned in the brightest light beyond comprehension—a light that we cannot even imagine or describe. The Almighty God comes forth from the tomb. The Son of God rose victorious from the dead!

"He walked with the disciples on the way to Emmaus and they did not recognize Him and He recounted for them Holy Scripture from the time of Moses that pertained to Him. When they got to Emmaus He broke the bread, and they recognized Him. Later the disciples said, "Did not our hearts burn within us as he talked to us on the road and explained the scriptures to us?" (Lk 24:32). Are not our hearts burning within us? For He is alive! In every word of the Scriptures and in every word of the Holy Sacrifice of the Mass, He is present to us. God gives Himself as a gift to us. Are not our hearts burning within us that God gives Himself to us? The all powerful God loves us so much that He came to this earth and He rose on the third day so that we could share in His life. He gives Himself to us this day in the Holy Eucharist. Are not our hearts burning within us? This is reality! The unseen is really real. He no longer walks this earth, but He lives in each of us."[16]

# Act of Consecration

Lord Jesus, Chief Shepherd of the Flock, I consecrate my priestly life to Your Heart, pierced on Calvary for love of us. From Your pierced Heart the Church was born, the Church You have called me as a priest, to serve in a most special way. You reveal Your Heart as symbol of Your love in all its aspects, including Your most special love for me, whom You have chosen as Your priest-companion. Help me always to pour out my life in love of God and neighbor. Heart of Jesus, I place my trust in You!

Dear Blessed Virgin Mary, I consecrate myself to your maternal and Immaculate Heart, this Heart which is symbol of your life of love. You are the Mother of my Savior. You are also my Mother. You love me with the most special love as this unique priest-son. In a return of love I give myself entirely to your motherly love and protection. You followed Jesus perfectly. You are His first and perfect disciple Teach me to imitate you in the putting on of Christ. Be my motherly intercessor so that, through your Immaculate Heart, I may be guided to an ever closer union with the pierced Heart of

Jesus, Chief Shepherd of the Flock, who leads me to the Father in the Holy Spirit.

# Letters

We thank all those who have taken the time to write to us. We very much appreciate your letters. Space limitations permit us to publish only a few of these:

Dear Fr. Carter,

I just received my first newsletter, *Shepherds of Christ.* I am very grateful for this publication. It provides some wonderful reflections and it is possible to read them even with a busy parish schedule.

Thank you for providing this wonderful service. Please accept the enclosed donation as a token of my appreciation.

Gratefully,
Rev. Gregory F. Hoppough, C.S.S.
Sacred Heart Church
Waltham, Massachusetts

As we are establishing the newsletter in an increasing number of countries, we are beginning to receive letters from our brother priests in different parts of the world. This helps all of us to be more aware of our fraternal union with all priests throughout the Universal Church. Here is a letter from a priest in Uganda, Africa:

Dear Father,

I am writing you to thank you for a well-done job for the renewal and growth of priests through the spirituality newsletter, *Shepherds of Christ.* I am also grateful for the copy I received recently, the Nov/Dec 1995 issue. How I wish I had received all issues. The articles are nourishing, supportive, informative and challenging. Thank you very much for your work and generosity.

I am wondering whether it is possible for me to continue receiving a copy of *Shepherds of Christ* regularly. As a person involved in giving renewal courses for priests, seminarians, and religious men and women, I have found it helpful.

Fr. Albert Gavamukulyo
Kisubi, Uganda

NOTES:
1. Scriptural quotations are taken from *The Jerusalem Bible,* Doubleday & Co.
2. *Bonaventure,* tr. by E. Cousens, Paulist Press, pp. 134-135.
3. *The Documents of Vatican II,* "Constitution on the Sacred Liturgy," America Press Edition, No. 5.

4. Ibid., "Pastoral Constitution on the Church in the Modern World," No. 3.

5. Karl Rahner, *Foundations of Christian Faith*, Seabury Press, p. 389.

6. John Cardinal Henry Newman, *Discourses Addressed to Mixed Congregations*, Longmans, Green and Co., pp. 111-112.

7. Pope John Paul II, as in *Set Apart for Service*, St. Paul Editions, pp. 197-199.

8. Donald Thorman, as in *The National Catholic Reporter*, February 9, 1973.

9. *The Documents of Vatican II*, "Constitution on the Sacred Liturgy," op. cit., No. 10.

10. Archbishop Joseph M. Raya, *The Face of God*, God With Us Publications, p. 40.

11. "Eucharistic Prayer IV," as in *The Vatican II Weekday Missal*, St. Paul Edition, p. 866.

12. Ibid., p. 891.

13. *Supplement to the Divine Office for the Society of Jesus*, published by the English Province of the Society of Jesus, pp. 21-22.

14. Fr. Edward Carter, S.J., *The Pain and the Joy*, Faith Publishing, pp. 5-7.

15. Pope Paul VI, *Devotion to the Blessed Virgin Mary*, United States Catholic Conference, Nos. 46 and 47.

16. Rita Ring, *Rosaries from the Hearts of Jesus and Mary*, to be published by Shepherds of Christ Publications.